MW01088666

LET ME LIVE IN PEACE!

The Live of Col. Charles Cessna

2nd Edition

By

C. W. Cissna

Privately Published
June 2012
January 2022
June 2023
Albuquerque

ISBN-13: 978-1477582954

ISBN-10: 1477582959

Available at Amazon.com

"If you teach them where they come from, they won't need as much help finding where they are going!"
Cordelia Carothers "Aunt Dee" Geoghegan (1894-1987)

Introduction

What follows is a fictionalized account of the life of Colonel Charles Cessna. Dates and major events are based on references from official documents. All the key persons mentioned are true historical characters.

Obviously, no one recorded their conversations. And almost never did they share with us the motives behind their choices. Those parts of this story are fiction.

Mixing fact with fiction helps us get an understanding of the real person.

From 1718 till 1800 the Cessna Family lived through six wars with Native Americans. In this book you will find references to tribal people and slaves using the terminology which fits into the context of that period.

The attitudes about race expressed by our ancestors three hundred years ago, in no way represent the convictions of this author.

Bcissna@aol.com

Books for Researchers
Available at Amazon.com

House of Cessna, Book One: The earliest research by Howard Cessna, completed in 1903, has been reproduced. Much newer research has been included.

House of Cessna, Book Two: Howard Cessna's work "House of Cessna, Second Series" published in 1935, is reprinted here. Some newer information is included.

House of Cessna, Book Three: A report of research done in France. Research there is far from complete.

Early Cessna Farms: References and maps locating most of the Cessna farms established between 1739 and 1820.

Our Cessna Legacy: Analytical Biography of Major John Cessna, with maps and 383 official records.

Reconstructed Census: A cautionary recreation of the family's first century in America. (Subject to revision as we continue researching.)

Muster Call: A partial anthology of family members who have served in U. S. Military.

Our Fifteen Minutes: Two hundred-fifty years of humorous, sad, and inspiring newspaper articles spotlighting family members in their moments of fame and infamy.

Tri-Centennial Celebration and Cessna Reunion. Outline of the 2018 National Cessna Reunion, and a guide for visiting the family's historical sites in Bedford.

Cessnas Gather: A summary report and journal of the 2018, From the three hundred year National Cessna Reunion.

Those Who Rest at Woods Cemetery: 2018 Survey of Wood's Cove Methodist Protestant Cemetery in Rainsburg, PA; matched with obituaries for Cessna Family members.

OUR AMERICA SERIES:
A history of America through
fictionalized accounts of the lives of family member
Available at Amazon.com

Bury My Children in a Strange Land. Huguenot refugee, Jean Le Cesna, transplanted his family to America's wilderness in 1718.

The Reluctant American. Joseph Cissna survived 5 years of captivity of with the Ottawa, six Indian Wars, and the American Revolution.

Forgotten Courage. Stephen Cessna/Cissna was among the first men to volunteer in the American Revolution. He was among the first men who enlisted in the Continental Army.

Let Me Live in Peace. A chronicle of the struggles and successes of Col. Charles Cessna, the highest ranking Cessna during the American Revolutionary military.

Tomahawks and Teacups. Jonathan Cessna was kidnapped and adopted by the Ottawa during the French and Indian War. He later died fighting with Daniel Boone in Ohio.

Will This Country Survive? The War of 1812 is described as it was experienced by the various members of our Cessna Family.

Where Can We Prosper? The children of Capt. Evans Cessna survive numerous epidemics and financial recessions of the new country from 1810 to 1860.

A Nation and Family Divided. An anthology of 84 members of this family who fought on both sides of the Civil War.

Civilizing a Pioneer Generation. After the Civil War, frontier Sheriff, George Sisney, faced down one of the Bloodiest Vendettas in American History. US Indian Agent, James Cisney, investigated the massacre at Wounded Knee and prevented a new Indian War.

CHAPTER ONE
18 July 1757

There was danger in every direction he looked. And he was looking hard in every direction.

"Something Is Not Right! I don't like this."

"What?" asked John. He had heard those words from his brother many times before. This morning, however, they held a much more ominous tone.

John paused to think more about their situation. *This does seem like a good way to catch an arrow...or a bullet,* he agreed to himself.

Charles had been anxious all morning. To be honest, John Cessna was just as anxious about this situation. But he was the older brother. He could not let the younger ones know he was afraid.

There were four young men working in the wheat harvest that July morning. It was not yet 10 AM. Already the heat was growing unbearable. But no matter how hot it was, the grain had to be cut and stacked before it could shatter. When it grew dry enough, the kernels would fall to the ground, making it impossible to gather.

John was the leader of this group. There was another group not far away, working on the next field. In the mind of John Cessna Jr. neither group had any business being out there that morning.

This war with the French and their Indians allies had started two years earlier, in the fall of 1755. It showed no sign of lessening. Danger was all around them.

General Braddock had marched his army to capture Fort Duquesne at the head of the Ohio River. Suffering a terrible defeat, he had managed to get himself and over 1000 people killed. Many of them were women and children. He had underestimated the power of the native peoples.

Almost immediately, those victorious warriors declared war on every English family in the colonies. Passing over the Allegheny mountains they began to slaughter isolated farm families. South-central Pennsylvania was a war zone.

That is where the Cessna family lived. And it is why these men were in a field, about 7 miles west of Shippensburg, on a hot July day.

During the summer of 1756, over 500 settlers had been killed. All were doing the very same thing that John and Charles Cessna were doing now. They were trying to get their harvest in, without enough guards to keep them safe.

John, Charles, and the others with them, were in constant danger of being attacked at any moment!

This particular field belonged to the Kirkpatrick family. They were immediate neighbors to the northwest, and close friends of the Cessna family. John Kirkpatrick Jr. was with the two Cessna brothers. A younger Cessna brother was there also.

John Cessna Jr. was the oldest at age 31. His two brothers (by his father's second marriage) were Charles age 17, and Evans, 14. The fourth member of the group was Kirkpatrick Jr. who had just turned 18 years old.

As the oldest, John Cessna was in charge.

John Cessna had served as an ensign in the militia for several years. He had experience in fighting the Indians and defending his neighbors. It was his responsibility to keep the younger men safe.

Their fathers and three younger brothers were working a short distance from them in a neighboring wheat patch. That field was owned by the Cessna family.

The groups were separated from view by a large patch of brush. They could hear each other. But at that particular hour neither could see the other group.

In the second field worked John Cessna Sr., a hired man named Dennis O'Neiden, and John Kirkpatrick Sr. It was their decision which had brought all of them out into the fields that day. The harvest couldn't wait.

Three young boys; Joseph (10) and Jonathan Cessna (7), and Joseph Kirkpatrick (7), worked alongside their fathers. It was their task to stack the wheat after the adults had cut it. It was arduous work. All of it was done with hand tools and by back breaking labor.

Despite numerous warnings from town folk and the militia officers, Cessna and Kirkpatrick had led their children into harm's way. Though all of the grown men were worried, Charles Cessna was the first to voice his concern. The others worked silently, so as to keep their fear in check.

Only the three youngest boys seemed unconcerned about the danger. They spent the morning making games of their work.

Charles' words only added to the caution which was eating at John Cessna the Junior. "What is bothering you now?"

Charles Cessna took a deep breath. "Well, first of all, everybody is focused on the work. Only Evans is keeping watch, and he has never done this before. And no one is keeping a look-out in the other field.

"And" he continued. "Evans is in the wrong place. If I was an Indian, I would sneak along the bottom of the creek over there. If he came through the woods we would see him pretty clearly. But if he came up below the creek bank, we wouldn't see him till he was 50 feet from us."

John Jr. stopped long enough to think through what Charles was saying.

He decided he ought to send Evans over to the high place on the creek bank. From there, he would be able to see a long way up the stream.

"Evans," he called. But time suddenly stopped for all of them. A loud crack stopped every heart. From the next field, six rifle shots rang out, in rapid sequence.

Immediately, the four young men dropped their harvest tools and dashed the 20 yards to where they had left their rifles. It was suddenly obvious that they had left their weapons much too distant from themselves.

From the next field, they could hear at least a dozen native voices screaming out terrifying war cries. John Jr. knew what this meant.

Charles was the first to reach his rifle and began to run towards the horrifying sounds. John raced after him and pushed him to the ground.

Charles looked up in shock.

"Don't rush in till we know what has happened," John hissed. All four men grabbed their guns and powder horns and ran to the thickest part of the brush. They struggled to see through the branches.

What they saw from that position made their stomachs turn. Evans fell to his knees and lost his breakfast.

In the next field, more than twenty warriors had circled their family. John was sure he had only heard six rifles fire. Now he knew there were many more weapons primed and ready to be used.

As they watched, the bodies of John Kirkpatrick Sr., and Dennis O'Neiden were scalped and stripped of their clothing. One of the savages hacked a number of times at Dennis' body, mutilating it horribly. He was sending a message to whoever might find it.

Cessna Sr. was bleeding from his head as the Indians tied his hands and pushed him ahead of them. The three young boys were left unbound, but pushed to follow the older man.

All of this happened in less than two minutes. The younger men had reached their hidden position just in time to see the scalping and their family members being pushed into the forest.

Two men were dead. Four captives had vanished into the tree line in less than four minutes.

Charles Cessna and the junior Kirpatrick jumped up and made as if to run around the brush and attack the invaders. John Cessna had to forcefully block their way.

"Don't be stupid! There are too many of them! You will only add your blood to the field." John insisted. "Besides, if you run out there now, they will just kill and scalp the rest of them."

It was something John Cessna had seen before. If people surrendered quickly enough, they would be taken captive. Being captive meant there was a chance of escaping or being rescued.

But if people resisted, or tried to fight back, their life ended with a quick blow from a tomahawk. The warriors were just as happy with taking a scalp.

The younger men could only see the terrible scene in front of them. John Cessna saw lessons from the past. Ten years of serving in militia taught John Cessna that the warriors were after the reward for scalps and prisoners offered by the French. Live prisoners brought a higher bounty.

And live prisoners could be made to carry whatever they had stolen on the raid. This was only beneficial if the captives were cooperative.

There was a chance that his father and brothers might yet be saved. Allowing them to be taken captive was the kindest and wisest option.

But it made no sense to the teenagers. As soon as the war party was out of sight, the three younger men turned their anger on John.

"How could you let them just run off with out trying?"

"What kind of coward are you."

"Shut up and follow me," John Jr. snapped. "There were too many of them. We need help. Evans, you run to Culbertson Fort. It is about a mile up Muddy Run. Tell them to bring everyone they can.

"You two come with me. We are going to follow them to see which way they go. There is a half dozen ways up over North Mountain. We need to know which way they go."

In less than ten minutes from the first shot, both fields were empty except for two bodies.

Fifty-eight year old John Cessna Sr. and three boys were running for their lives through the forest. Evans was running as fast as he could for help from the Culbertson family. The three remaining men were following the war party as cautiously as they could. They dared not risk being seen.

Although, outwardly, John Cessna Jr. was stoic and resolved; on the inside he was cursing his father. They should have waited until the common guard could come with them. Fifty men had a much better chance than four men and five boys.

But his father had not wanted to wait his turn. Every farmer in the valley needed their fields harvested as soon as possible. Cessna and Kirkpatrick were supposed to wait their turn.

Being impatient had proven to be disastrous for these two families.

CHAPTER TWO
The Pursuit

The pursuit by these three young men was driven from desperate concern for their family.

It was Charles who found a bright drop of blood on a leaf. He announced that someone ahead of them was wounded. Silently, he showed the crimson drop to John Kirkpatrick. Charles was at a loss for what to do next. He turned in desperation to John.

John Jr. was calculating their situation in between his deliberate panting. He could not afford to get winded right now. He focused on pacing himself. He willed his body and brain to work together.

There are only three of us, and a LOT more of them. What will we do if we catch them? We ain't soldiers or injun fighters. Hell, Charles can barely shoot a gun. Maybe if we stay close enough an opportunity will present itself.

John Cessna Jr. took note that the raiding party had stayed about 50 yards inside the edge of the forest. They were skirting around other farms, looking for any more targets of opportunity.

This looked promising. Sometimes war parties left their prisoners with only one or two guards while they attacked a new place. There may just be a chance!

At some point he realized the warriors were no longer heading south around the mountain.

They were looking for the pass over it. Changing direction, he took his brothers north, he ran through the thick undergrowth, directly towards the pass. *We might have a chance to get ahead of them,* he reasoned.

They picked up the trail right where John predicted. The summer before, he and a group of militia had chased another war party up this same trail. The marauders had climbed up the steep path to cross the mountain.

Now reason began to catch up with the three young men. Kirkpatrick was the one who offered the most sobering thought.

"You know, most of the Culbertsons are off with the militia guarding people's fields. That bunch is supposed to be east of Shippensburg. That is 10 or 12 miles from here. It is going to be a long time before Evans can get help."

"We need more people," said John in a firm voice. We can't attack that large a party."

After a quick check they realized they only had 10 rounds of ammunition between the three of them. It would not be much of a fight, even if they had known how to fight.

"We can't give up now," Charles insisted. "Maybe if we just lay back and follow them we can at least see where they go."

Not willing to yield leadership to his brother this time, Charles started climbing the path again. Having won this challenge for authority, the others followed him.

"Tomorrow we can bring the militia back and catch them." Charles called back at them.

At the top of the pass they learned that the group had separated. The boys had been taken down the mountain's west side. Another group had followed the ridge top north-east. Footprints told them that their father had gone with the second group.

John Cessna spoke the obvious. Their brothers were heading west towards the Delaware town of Kittanning. Their father was headed north towards the Iroquois lands in New York. It would be foolish for the three of them to follow two different paths.

The further they got from their home, and the deeper they got into the woods, the more vulnerable each of the young men began to feel. Their courage faded as their blood cooled.

Anger, and a need to protect their family had driven them this far. Now their bravery was replaced with fear for their own lives. Their pace slowed as much from cooled passion as from exhaustion at climbing the mountain trail.

They paused, pacing silently in circles. Three choices lay in the footprints before them: west, north, or back home. None of them spoke. It was as though saying the words "We need to go back" would be admitting defeat and cowardice.

But three defeated hearts did climb back down from North Mountain. They bypassed their own farms. No one was there anyway. Their mothers and other siblings had been moved to the safety of town many weeks earlier.

Instead the young men took the most direct route back to town. The responding company of the militia met them just 2 miles short of town. It was too late for them to help in any way except to bury the dead.

CHAPTER THREE
Shippensburg

The tragic irony of that July day is that the Cessna family were not really farmers.

John Cessna Sr. had been one of the pioneer settlers of Shippensburg. In 1739 it had been just a cluster of cabins along a path that led from Colonial Pennsylvania to remote trading posts in the wilderness. The wilderness was still owned by Indians.

From this point on, wagons were unable to negotiate the narrow trails and steep mountain passes. All trade goods headed for the West had to be transferred from wagons to packhorses. All of the furs coming from the West had to be moved from horses into wagons.

John Cessna Sr. had first chosen a town lot in the busiest part of the village. He had started with a store. But by 1757 the family business had expanded to a blacksmith shop, and a place where teamsters could rest while feeding themselves and their animals.

Cessna also had several packhorses for sale or hire. He would often buy sick or lame horses cheap. After nursing them back to health, he sold them at a good profit.

It was not until 1750 that John Cessna Sr. decided to diversify by adding two farms. They were about 7 miles west of town. These were used to grow grain and hay. He could sell this at his businesses. Some of the grain was also converted to whiskey for his tavern.

One of the farms was managed by his daughter Mary and her husband, Andrew Neal. The other by his oldest son, John Jr. This was their father's way of helping the two children of his first marriage get a good start in life.

Just before moving to Shippensburg in 1739, John Sr. had taken a second wife, Agnes Campbell. The children by this marriage were all more than 15 years younger than John Jr.

As the first born, John Cessna Jr. was responsible for helping provide for his father's new family. But his stepmother was just a few years older than himself. This proved to be awkward at times. His father's disappearance was going to be one of those uncomfortable occasions.

Charles Cessna was the first born of the second marriage. At age 17, he was surprisingly mature for his age. Having a much older and wiser brother was appreciated by Charles.

There would be no evening meal in the Cessna home that night. The house was part inn, part tavern, part home. There were always paying guests mingled with the large Cessna family. That night, the house was filled by noisy people processing the tragedy. A large crowd of neighbors had come to offer support.

Women lamented about what would become of the family now. Men gnawed over who was to blame for the tragedy.

"John" said one of four men who had surrounded the oldest son. "You are the man of the house now. It's up to you to pull this place together."

They showered the boy with all of the clichés deemed appropriate for such occasions. They offered him their support, but tempered it with cautions of "don't get foolish now."

Charles and Evans watched as the men held an informal, but sacred, ceremony. They transferred the mantle of family leadership onto the eldest son. From his disheartened state, Charles was grateful not to be in that position.

The stone house, which was the heart of the Cessna family businesses, spent most of its life as a gathering place. It provided temporary shelter for the teamsters. These men moved merchandise from the cities in the east to the trading posts in the west.

The house always smelled of strangers and hard living. The family's private quarters in the back room and loft were small. The daughters slept with their parents. The sons slept overhead.

The great room provided space for as many as twelve men to sleep on the floor in front of the fireplace. Two long tables and benches provided a place for them to eat.

There were four teamsters seeking shelter that evening. They recognized that the family was in great distress. All of them quietly eased out of the building, leaving Agnes Cessna with her remaining children.

She was beside herself.

Without filtering any of her fears, she verbally analyzed the desperateness of their situation. The children were deeply terrified by her panic. Agnes alternated between anger and uncontrollable weeping.

At some point the fire was banked and the family began to bed down. In the small hours of morning, Charles and John took charge of tucking the younger ones into their sleeping pallets. Two pallets were empty.

Mother's cries were the only voice heard in a dark house of sleepless bodies. Somewhere towards the middle of their sleep her crying stopped.

"They are coming back!" she announced to the darkness. "All of them!"

And with those words, the crying ended for good. Every child knew without being told that this was the new reality they would mutually agree to. No debate. No doubt. They were coming back!

Mother had decided that this was the assumption about the future. This is how the family would operate. If you had any doubt it should remain in your own mind, and never be spoken aloud.

They were coming back!

CHAPTER FOUR
Live Goes On

The next morning, the children were awakened to Agnes preparing the first meal of the day. She sounded as though nothing had happened previous afternoon. One by one they emerged from sleeping places and drifted to the table.

The Cessna family was prosperous but not wealthy. When they were old enough to feed themselves, Father had seen that each new child was furnished with a pewter plate and spoon.

It was not luxury, but it was better than the wooden platters used by the visiting teamsters. Each plate had its own distinctive markings. This was not a set of dishes so much as a collection of individualized place settings.

The settings for Father, Jonathan, and Joseph were not on the table. The plate for John Jr. lay at the end of the table where Father's had been yesterday. Charles and Evans found their plates were on either side of his.

Mother was at the far end, ready to give the list of chores for that day. It was she who decided what needed to be done. Breakfast was the family business meeting. John would have the responsibility of making assignments and choosing who had which tasks. Charles could see that his older brother was uneasy with the burden.

John was the first to speak. "We need to join the common guard."

"No" said mother firmly.

In a shaky voice, Charles said, "Yes, we must. It won't do us any good to save ourselves if the town burns down around us."

The younger children were unable to speak. William and the girls began to cry as they watched this drama of power play out at the table. None were surprised to see that John and Charles agreed on the issue.

"It is the only way we will ever get our harvest in," offered Charles in support of his brother. "Shippensburg has more men than guns. So every gun is needed. Paw would skin us if we let someone else use our rifles."

They could tell their mother was in a great quandary. Sending her sons back into danger was unthinkable. But Agnes knew that danger would come for them anyway if they did nothing. The feeling of having no place to be safe was a horrible experience for a mother.

"Maybe we should leave Evans here with one of the guns." suggested Charles. "He can protect the house here, while you and I do our part with the guard.

"And besides," he continued. "Fort Franklin is only a hundred yards away. Mother, you can move the other children into the fort if there is trouble."

The tiny stockade was already crowded with refugees from the fighting. A hundred people were camping on the small lawn. It was uncomfortable. But with four soldiers at the gate, it offered some safety.

After a few minutes of further discussion, John made his first decision as *man of the house.*

Evans would stay with one of the three remaining guns. Together, Evans and mother would try to manage serving the teamsters.

Mother and the smaller children would stay close to the stone house, and return to a normal routine. Of course normal meant a full day of trying to turn plants and animals into something of value. These things could provide them with food and resources for the coming winter. There was never an end to the things which needed doing.

Chores would continue as usual until Father and the boys returned. Mother was certain they were coming back. The business would continue to operate. Just not very efficiently in the absence of their father.

Eventually, the Cessna's got their wheat harvested. The workers had returned to the task with a greater sense of urgency and completed everyone's fields much quicker than they had thought possible.

Out of a overwhelming guilt, John Cessna Jr. insisted that the Kirkpatrick farm be harvested ahead of theirs. The Cessna field would be the very last one for that season.

In the end, John estimated that over 40% of the crop had been lost because of the delay. Father had been right to worry, but wrong not to accept the loss.

Now father's absence began to be felt from a new direction. Shippensburg, like most frontier towns, operated on a very elaborate system of bartering. Few people had actual cash to trade for the goods and services they needed.

John Cessna Sr. had been adept at negotiating the system. He always had a number of trades going on at any one time.

John was a master at swapping one resource for another, then trading it *down the road* for yet another. He might make a series of 10 trades, each increasing his value, until he was able to exchange the final item for a bit of cash.

And of course he was not above trading for something against the promise of a future benefit. John Cessna owed dozens of small debts. He had even more small debts owed to him. None of which were written down. It seemed the people who owed him now felt that his absence meant their obligations had been erased.

Charles assumed leadership in this arena. He had paid close attention to his father's business deals. Of all the boys, he had studied his father's negotiating skills and practices. All transactions may be written in their Father's head...but copies of nearly every one of them also existed in Charles' memory.

Men of the community were surprised when Charles Cessna presented himself to collect a debt owed by them to his father. They had hoped it was forgotten. But seventeen year old Charles Cessna was now standing there to remind them they had promised a half bushel of wheat against drinks which Father had served them back in the Winter.

Francis Campbell was even more surprised when Charles showed up bringing a half dozen pullets which his father had promised against two peck of apples.

As near as his mother could tell, not one of his Father's business deals had gone uncompleted. The family treasury continued to get bigger in tiny increments of a shilling here and a pence there.

Agnes developed a new sense of appreciation for the acumen of her oldest son, Charles.

John Cessna Jr. was in a predicament. He was now thirty-one. He had been planning to take a wife. He had almost convinced his father that he was ready. If this had been a good harvest his plans would be secure. John had planned to build a cabin on the very farm where they had been attacked.

Sarah Rose had been his "intended" for a year now. The Rose family lived north of town. The Indian War had delayed their plans. They were now living among the refugees in Fort Franklin.

Now, his father's absence meant Junior already had a large family to care for. The loss of the harvest meant he didn't have enough money to take a wife and build a home. The dream of starting a family of his own seemed to be fading more each day.

Charles sensed the dilemma. He urged John to continue his plans for a wedding. "We can't possibly care for both the farm and the tavern. Father was overreaching. You and Sarah should take the farm on Muddy Run. I'll see that the tavern provides a living for mother and the others."

Plans were made for John and Sarah to marry on Christmas Day in 1757. Mother was convinced that their father and the boys would be home by then.

Charles had been successful enough that they could pay the quit rents on both of the farms and the house in Shippensburg. Charles was even managing to keep the shelves of their store filled with goods, ready for eager travelers. Business was good.

Wealth on the frontier was built in small increments of shillings, or an extra half-bushel of grain. Charles did not let the pace slip one bit. The family's wealth continued to nudge forward.

His youth did not escape most of the men in the community. More than one tried to take advantage of his lack of negotiating experience; only to find that he was just as stubborn as his father. He was perhaps more astute. Charles never traded for anything that he did not already have a market for.

CHAPTER FIVE
Elizabeth

In early November Charles made a critical visit to the Culbertson family. Captain Alexander Culbertson was among the earliest casualties of this war. In April of 1756, Culberson had been killed at the Battle of Sideling Hill.

Now, Culbertson's widow and children had moved into town for safety. They were living in a borrowed house, just a few doors from his own.

Among the several debts which his father had owed was a small one to Alex Culbertson. Culbertson had one of the more dependable Still-Houses in the area, and the Cessna Tavern was a regular customer for his whiskey.

And Charles thought that this family might need that money during this challenging time. His own family's struggle without a father made him more sympathetic.

Mrs. Culbertson was greatly surprised as the young man put coins in her hand. He seemed so young to be carrying such responsibility. Her tears were enough thanks for him as he turned to head home.

But a sweet voice halted his departure. "Mr. Cessna, may I ask you something?"

At age thirteen, Elizabeth Culbertson was three and a half years younger than himself. Calling him "Mr." should have seemed inappropriate. But both of these children had been transformed into adults by the losses their families had suffered in war.

Charles and Elizabeth were on the verge of adulthood, being rapidly pushed towards it by the tragic loss of their fathers. Adolescence is a luxury that frontier people cannot afford. Everyone grew up fast.

"I wonder if I might have your help with selling something," Elizabeth asked quite coyly.

Charles was always intrigued with any prospect of selling or bartering. This captured his attention completely.

Charles Cessna had previously been smitten by Abigail Martin, and in his mind he assumed that she was the girl he would marry... maybe...in about ten years. Abigail lived in Carlisle, about 20 miles to the east. Before the war began, the Cessna family made regular trips to the county seat. They had a monthly reunion there with his Uncle Stephen Cessna's family.

Seeing each other once a month had seemed a perfect relationship for Charles. He did not have to bother with paying frequent attention to a girl. And the four weeks between courtship sessions, gave him lots of time to build adventurous stories to entertain the girl.

He had not been able to see Abigail in two years, because of this war.

If he were honest with himself, it completely escaped Charles Cessna's awareness that any of the girls in Shippensburg might be interested in him. He had already surveyed the landscape. It seemed to him that the hometown girls were much too shallow for him to consider as a partner.

However, living on a remote farm, the Culbertson girl had escaped his attention. She had not gotten into town very much. Because of the current war, she lived full time in the village.

Charles, however, had not escaped her attention. Elizabeth had calculated very carefully how she might orchestrate their first meeting.

She held a packet of paper envelopes in front of her bosom for him to view. Each one had been tied tightly and carefully. A bundle of about two dozen were then tied with a ribbon.

Much of her bosom was in view as well.

Charles was curious. He was also distracted. Until that moment he had not realized that this girl even had a bosom. Now she had her hands cupped in front of it, tightly holding the packet of folded brown paper.

She was no longer the little child who followed around his friends Sam and James Culbertson. She was on the cusp of womanhood.

"I have some Kitchen Garden Seeds I want to sell." Elizabeth said. In his mind the girl had been instantly transformed. Never again would he think of her by the childish moniker "Lizzie."

"Widow Piper handles a market for garden seeds at her tavern." Charles offered. "She might be interested in buying them from you."

"No, I already spoke to her." Elizabeth said with her sweetest charm. She projected a damsel-in-distress tone in her plea. Charles was completely unaware that he had been affected. His mind was already focused on business.

"Widow Piper only sells seeds one variety at a time," the girl continued. "I want to sell these as a lot. Mother and I have been working on the perfect Kitchen Garden for many years now."

Charles smiled. He thought it humorous that the young girl was claiming a long history of gardening experience.

But he admitted that Mrs. Culbertson was famous for the table she set from her garden. He agreed that this family was well known for its special talents in that area.

Charles also noted that this girl was avoiding looking him directly in the eyes. He wondered what she might be hiding.

"I have planned the perfect Kitchen Garden for any wife." Elizabeth said the word "wife" with an intriguing lilt. And as intended, the young merchant was intrigued. He tried to catch her eye, but she turned away in a blush.

"This is every seed a woman needs to grow a garden. They will yield fresh vegetables from early Spring until the snows come. There are 20 varieties of vegetables and 5 kinds of herbs. And there is a chart showing how to lay out everything in a plot, and when it is best to plant them."

Elizabeth was quite proud of herself. "Everything you need for the perfect garden is in one bundle, right here."

Charles was impressed on many levels. This neatly tied packet was beginning to take on some value in his eyes. He began to recognize her marketing concept.

Charles was also slowly becoming aware...that he was aware...of the blossoming charms she was using as a backdrop for the merchandise. Noticing the direction of his stare, Elizabeth offered an approving smile.

Most farm families kept a remarkably simple garden. It might hold seven or eight varieties of vegetables. These were chosen to supplement their simple meals. Most were root vegetables used to add bulk to stews and soups.

At the Cessna home, as with most pioneer homes, the evening meal usually consisted of a stew made in the large pot hanging in the fireplace. Whatever meat and vegetables were available from that day were added to what was left from the day before. These were then boiled until they were a mushy texture.

This was the most efficient way of distributing the small amounts of meat among all those at the table. One squirrel or one rabbit (and sometimes both) could feed 8 or more people this way.

There was seldom any companion food other than bread. Every meal was one course. Apple cider was the only drink for children. Apple Jack, beer, or whiskey quenched the thirsty men.

Lacking any spices other than coarse salt, each day's meal varied little in flavor from the meal of the night before. It all came from the same pot. It all came from the same Kitchen Garden. It was just basic food.

Still, Charles knew that wealthier families tried to offer more refined fare. Meat and vegetables were served in separate courses and offered with a variety of seasonings. But this took a more sophisticated kind of planning by the woman of the house. It required more than just gathering wild herbs and spices.

Widow Piper's tavern served meals like that. The travelers who stayed at the Cessna Tavern filled their bellies with a simpler fare.

The concept of planning an entire garden for the sake of variety at the table, showed a very clever kind of "forward thinking" on the part of this young girl. Charles was impressed, to say the least.

Then, it happened.

He stepped back just half a step, as though he were leaving. To hold his attention girl suddenly turned her face towards him. At last he saw her eyes. They were magical.

They were not brown...but not green. *Hazel?* He asked himself. *No, they are several colors at the same time.* He tried to commit the image to his memory. But the hue of her eyes was so unique he had nothing to match it with.

When she turned her head he noticed something else. A charming little mole was hiding just behind, and below her left ear. It never dawned on him that she had turned deliberately so he might notice this fascinating feature. Elizabeth had purposefully captured his curiosity. No wild creature in the forest had ever fallen into a more clever trap.

The conversation continued for several minutes as they discussed some possibilities. The young man agreed to take the seed package on consignment and look for a market. He was even feeling excited about the prospect.

Elizabeth Culbertson felt triumphant. She had succeeded in enlisting this handsome young man as her ally. But she was proudest of finding an excuse for him to come see her on a frequent basis. The money would be nice as well.

"Thank you, Mr. Cessna" she said as he took the packets from her. She had pronounced "Mr. Cessna" in careful, deliberate, and tender tones. The musical way she said his name would linger on his mind for a long time.

CHAPTER SIX
December 1757

By the week before Christmas of 1757, the Cessna family had settled into its new paradigm of family leadership.

Charles Cessna would be 18 years old in a few weeks. Supported by his younger brother, Evan, he was now in charge of all family business except the stables. John would handle the animals...and the farm.

There was a wedding to plan. John Cessna Jr. had finally committed himself to take a wife, and Sarah Rose had accepted. He was 31 and she was 18.

The couple seemed happy. There was still a threat of war looming over the community. But John and Sarah had waited long enough. With his father *gone to the Indians*, there was longer any one to argue that they should wait longer.

The Fall and early weeks of the winter of 1757 were busy for Charles. There was a lot of business to conclude before the snow made traveling difficult.

On December 22nd, Charles spent the day 4 miles north of Shippensburg. The weather had turned cold and a neighbor was butchering three hogs for the winter.

Charles held a promise to one of the haunches. He was volunteering to help with the butchering just to make certain that his payment was *correct*. And true to his nature, he managed to further barter for one of the hog heads. The haunch would be carefully smoked and fed piecemeal to travelers at the Cessna Inn.

The head would join a wild turkey as a part of his brother's wedding feast. Charles could almost smell the steaming apple in its mouth.

Arriving in town Cessna was nearly frozen. But he was filled with pride at his profits for the day. Guiding his horse up King street, he noticed something was wrong! A crowd had gathered in front of the stone house.

Charles feared that it meant a new family tragedy, and rushed towards those he loved. In the center of a group of neighbors, stood a ragged man, hugging his mother.

"Paw!?"

By some miracle, his father had returned. He stood in front of a wondering family. Equally amazed, was the crowd of town folks. The new parson had found his Christmas Miracle for the holiday sermon.

John Cessna Sr. had managed to confuse his captors as to whether he was English or their French ally. Grandfather had been French and insisted that his sons learn their mother tongue.

Sold from one tribe to another, John Cessna had made his eventually escape. He had spent months walking his way back home. The ordeal left him starved and abused. But he returned to his home with a mostly unbroken spirit.

Jonathan and Joseph had vanished and would not be heard of again for five years. The Kirkpatrick boy was gone as well.

Agnes Cessna's prophecy had been partly fulfilled. Charles felt tremendous relief as the weight of his family was lifted from his shoulders.

In the weeks ahead he would educate his father on the progress which had been made in his absence. His father nodded approval at some of his actions, grunted disappointment at others. He left Charles in doubt as to whether the son had *done good* or not.

The task of supporting his family was shifted. That burden was lifted from his shoulders. But for some reason, his heart felt heavier instead of lighter. Charles slipped into an inexplicable depression. After carrying so much accountability for his family, not being needed seemed the worst thing that could happen to him. It left him feeling lost.

The wedding of John and Sarah Rose proceeded as planned. Charles' father now offered the farm on Muddy Run Creek to the oldest son. He would have to work on it for a while before he would be given title to it.

This was John Cessna Sr.'s plan for building a dynasty. He would purchase a farm as his sons grew old enough to marry, and place it in their care. At some point, usually after a mean spirited debate, he would allow the property to be placed in his child's name. It was a "gift" that must be wrestled away from the old man.

The Christmas wedding made a profound change in Charles as well. He had anticipated standing with pride beside his brother; knowing that his efforts had made this day possible. Now he stood in the back of the room as his father occupied the spot he should be filling. His father received the congratulatory compliments which Charles had earned.

He felt jealous that his brother was embarking on a new life. John Jr. had a new sense of purpose and responsibility. Charles was secretly bitter that he had lost the clear direction of his own life.

For half a year he had been a man. Now he was a child again. It did not taste sweet at all. Still, it made him feel guilty to think he regretted his father's return on any level.

Depression robbed him of any sensations of success from the past six months. This was his first real struggle with dejection. But it would be only the first of a lifetime of such experiences for him.

At age eighteen, Charles Cessna began to long for independence from his father. He began to dream of his own place, his own wife, and his own family. He had no intention of waiting as long as his brother had.

John Jr. had waited until he was in his thirties to start his own life. It was expected that a man would have his own farm and ample money before he could afford a wife. John Jr. had spent three decades under their father's dominance.

Charles Cessna had no intention of waiting that long. He was ready now!

CHAPTER SEVEN
The Council

"**W**hen you boys figure it all out, be sure to write it down so we can tell the King."

Lucinda Piper, set two fists of tankards in front of the Council of Public Opinions, and laughed as she swished away to her other chores. The old men of Shippensburg gathered regularly in her establishment. Though there were half a dozen inns in the small town, most catered to the rougher class of teamsters. Widow Piper set a more elegant table and her place was sought by merchants and government travelers.

And it was a favorite place for *The Council* to meet. They had no official authority over any town business. But they considered their meetings to be important, nonetheless. They usually arrived late in the morning after the overnight guests had departed.

The Widow's upscale accommodations gave an air of importance to their gathering. She offered China cups and plates. Instead of home dipped candles she had two oil lanterns. She also had some of the best ale in the village.

Despite her flirtations, the men understood that Widow Piper was not on the menu. Still, her flirtation had a way of making them feel significant.

This council had an auspicious beginning two years earlier. None other than Benjamin Franklin and his son William had come to Shippensburg, and asked to confer with *the leading men*. His invitation had promoted these gray haired merchants and farmers to the status of "leading men."

Dr. Franklin was well known among the population as the inventor of the lightening rod. Every cabin and barn in Cumberland Valley now wore one of these new inventions designed to protect from violent thunderstorms.

Franklin was also well known as a strong voice in public defense. He used his paper, the Pennsylvania Gazette, to inform and warn the population. During the 1740s Franklin had convinced the people of Penn's Colony to create a temporary military force called the "Associators." He had even organized a lottery to fund this militia.

At that time, the major threat had been from French, Spanish, and Portuguese ships which sailed up the Delaware and Susquehanna Rivers to raid the settlements. Two years ago he had been hoping to put some reason and organization into defense of the frontier against the Indian invaders. Franklin knew that Braddock's defeat was only the start of a long Indian War.

On that day, young Charles Cessna had stood invisible in a corner of the tavern as the Franklins argued with the locals. They proposed that Shippensburg should not wait for the King to send a professional army to protect them. They needed to build a fort and form a militia right now!

That was two years ago.

It was now nine months since that bloody day in the harvest field when Charles had been thrust into manhood. It was three months since he had been pushed back into childhood.

John Cessna Sr. had survived captivity. But his withered countenance sitting at the Widow's table was a testimony to the accuracy of Ben Franklin's prophecy.

Dr. Franklin was in Shippensburg again. Now he was pushing for men to volunteer for a new militia, and for teamsters to offer themselves for hire. General Forbes was organizing a new army. Come summer, he would march on Fort Duquesne.

The idea was not well received. Everyone remembered the massacre of Braddock's army in '55. It was that mess which had started all of these Indian raids in the first place.

The Council of Opinions insisted that too many men had already been lost from their town. To send more of their young fighters off to help the General would leave their homes more vulnerable.

Dr. Ben Franklin left Shippensburg that afternoon feeling unsure if he had been successful in his persuasion. He hoped to find a better reception in Carlisle.

Alexander Culbertson was one of the missing people. He had once been a strong voice on this council. His powerful voice was absent and sorely missed.

The father of Charles' new business partner, Captain Culbertson led one of the militia companies which Franklin had organized. Elizbeth's father now lay dead at the foot of Sideling Hill.

In April of 1756, Captain Culbertson had taken his company in pursuit of Shingas and a large group of Delaware warriors. A vicious two hour battle left the commander and 20 of the town people dead. Another 20 or so had returned to their homes severely wounded. Only 10 men returned to Shippensburg unscathed that day. It stunned the entire village.

Twenty men had died because they followed Franklin's guidance. Many felt that professional soldiers should be doing the fighting, not volunteers fresh from farm fields. Like many others in this town, Elizabeth Culbertson would be forever cheated by her father's death.

The local men continued to meet at the Widow Piper's and formed what would eventually become *The Committee of Public Safety*. Having spent months as a captive of the savages, John Cessna Sr. held an esteemed position on the council.

On the first day of April 1758, the group met again. Eighteen-year-old Charles Cessna arrived to stand before them with the newest copy of the Pennsylvania Gazette. It was the most official news to come from the east. He knew this group would be eager for its arrival.

Charles had already read it carefully from top to bottom. Charles Cessna held a secret that he dared not reveal. He was nearsighted.

He feared that it would limit how others thought about him. So when he was twelve years of age, he determined to keep it to himself. It limited his role in the community. He could not be a hunter or soldier. Even standing in the harvest field that day, rifle at ready, he was aware that he could not see details in the forest's edge as clearly as others could.

He had stood guard, watching for enemy in the woods. But he really could not see the woods well enough to spot them. He was too ashamed to admit it to those in charge.

Charles' mind became programmed to search for bits of information. It allowed him to project a much larger picture than most men could see with their eyes. The newspaper was his eyes.

Charles Cessna was considered as the *man in the know* on most topics. Especially for anything that was bigger than Cumberland County. Having the newspaper gave him a special perspective, or vision, of what was happening to their world.

"It's not knowing HOW they fight that is going to win this war," Charles interjected into the conversation. "It is knowing WHY they fight. When you understand why they fight; you can find a way to make them quit."

The conversation grew quiet.

Charles' contribution was out of place. He was far too young to be a member of this discussion. He was immediately embarrassed that he had spoken out.

"Kill enough of 'em and they will quit!" pronounced Will Campbell. "Once he is dead, it don't matter why an Indian went on the war path."

"Yeah, well they ain't all that easy to kill," offered John Cessna. "Just finding 'em before they find you is the hardest part."

James Duncan took a long slow draught of ale. He turned to the brash young man, and asked, "So, why do you think they are trying to kill us?"

"Remember when the French built Fort Duquesne, and George Washington went up there to *ask* them to leave?" Charles Cessna reminded them. He understood that his opinion was not very welcome. Still, he could not hold himself back any longer.

"Remember that Jumonville fella that got himself killed while he was Washington's prisoner? Mighty inconvenient it was, I say. Cause that is what started it all. France got so worked up they declared war on England!"

Dr. McCall contributed, "Yes, but them Delaware and Shawnee just looking for an excuse. They still think this valley belongs to them. Ain't nothing gonna make them ask for peace."

The leadership of Pennsylvania had been working feverously to make new treaties which would end the war. But there were just so many tribes and chiefs to negotiate with that it seemed impossible.

And each of the colonies was trying to make their own treaties. The entire process of quieting the native's anger seemed to be going nowhere. It certainly did not help that the French were out there paying for every scalp and prisoner brought in.

"Can't you see?" Will Campbell said in surprising agreement with the boy. "It ain't all these petty little gripes the Indians are giving Governor Denny. It is Fort Duquesne.

"As long as the French sit up there on Three Rivers, the war is going to continue. Someone has gotta make the French leave or the Indians ain't gonna go back to their homes."

Daniel Duncan offered, "Well General Braddock tried to do that and got himself buried in the woods. My boy is out there with him."

"Captain Culbertson and Francis Scott are out in those woods too." Someone added. In fact five of this group's former members now lie buried at scenes of battles around the county.

"Forbes is gonna try again this summer," John Montgomery reminded him. "This Scotsman is a bit smarter than that English prima donna." General Forbes was their newest, and probably their last, hope for turning the tide of this war.

The group began to talk over each other in efforts to get their opinions heard. The young Cessna boy was invisible once again.

At some point they returned their attention to the newspaper. Their focus landed on a report about a man named Peter Heydrich. It seemed a large number of Indians entered a small cove to raid and plunder.

Heydrich was able to see what was happening. He warned his neighbors to run to the block house of Martin Hess. As they made their escape to safety, Heydrich grabbed a drum and fife and disappeared into a large thicket on the hillside.

He alternated between beating the drum, playing the fife, and shouting orders to an imaginary army. Peter was able to confuse the Indians enough to delay their onslaught. He was able to save every one of his neighbors by this tactic.

"Three cheers for old Peter!" shouted Campbell and the entire group raised their tankards to their new hero.

"The Indians ain't too dumb. They don't like to come out to play unless they think they got the advantage in numbers and surprise" Montgomery stated.

"They won't march right out in front and let you shoot 'em like our Regulars do." And the group laughed together in the first light moment they had experienced in weeks.

Charles had only spoken one other time with this group. It was the day in August of 1757, when he read the article about "the massacres at Cisney and Steensen's fields."

With a heavy heart that day, he had read aloud the condemnation, "these people refused to join with their neighbors who had a guard appointed them, because they couldn't have their fields reaped the first."

It was a tough thing for a boy to read criticism of his father in the newspaper. Now Charles faded in the background once again. His father assumed the role of reading the news.

"Listen to this story about Mrs. Zellars," John Cessna Sr. said in his most authoritative voice. Once again, he had command of the conversation.

While her husband was off looking for Indians to fight, Christine Zellars had gotten her slaves to fortify their home. At the warning of Indians in the area, she locked her family away in the house, and retired to the basement. There, she opened one window and stood beside it with an axe in hand.

As one of the savages poked his head in to investigate the open window, she introduced him to her weapon. Pulling the body inside, she waited for the next curious head. In this way she was able to kill three members of the war party.

The Council of Public Opinion offered three cheers for the victorious Mrs. Zellars.

"Divide and conquer!" cried Charles Cessna. "That's the way." He was feeling very passionate that day. For the second time he had dared to interrupt his elders. It took both they and him by surprise.

The older men were stunned at the enthusiastic declaration of this presumptuous lad. Why was he still here? They were speechless. His father looked very embarrassed by his son's outburst.

"And just how are you gonna get the savages to line up in single file so you can shoot them one at a time?" asked Dunlap.

"They do it on their own. Every time they come raiding, they come over the mountain passes," Charles offered.

"When that group took paw and my brothers, they came over Tuscarora Mountain. That path is so narrow that there are at least a dozen places where they have to go in a single file. We can meet them as they come over."

The group grumbled a lot of "buts." Still, the wisdom of the boy's suggestions nagged at the back of their minds. Of course there was no way for this group to make such a proposal happen. So the Council resumed chewing the news into palatable bits which they could repeat in later conversations.

The boy was invisible again.

John Cessna Sr. had grown quiet. Charles' story had reminded him of the two sons he had lost that day in the harvest field.

John Cessna passed the paper to another reader. While his companions continued with their debate, he began to withdraw into self condemnation and guilt. Within a few minutes he was ready to leave. Making quiet goodbyes he left the tavern with his son in tow.

Charles knew he had embarrassed his father by speaking out of turn. His obvious failure to earn their respect had bruised his own ego as a result.

His father walked silently home, refusing to speak to the lad. Charles thought it was because the man was angry at him. He did not guess that John Cessna's heart was breaking. He had been reminded of the sons and lives he had lost on July 18th.

Charles Cessna knew a place where his own ego would be quickly healed. He made his way to the Culbertson home. He had managed to sell another pack of Kitchen Garden Seeds for Elizabeth. He was anxious to bring her the four shillings she had earned.

Charles would keep only 1 pence as his commission, a testimony to the other benefits he was drawing from this alliance. Elizabeth was delighted to see him.

Those eyes are mostly Hazel, he thought as he felt the warmth of her smiling face. He would never grow tired of the way she said his name.

"I knew I was wise in choosing you for this task, Mr. Cessna," she gushed. "You are clever enough to see how important it is to sell the seeds as a complete garden."

In fact, it had not been difficult to sell the seeds. It only needed finding the right buyer. He sold the first package of Elizabeth's seeds to a teamster. He happened to be complaining about what an unimaginative cook his wife was, and what a good cook Mrs. Cessna was. Charles was able to convince him that his wife would be the envy of Lancaster if she followed the garden's plan.

His next sale was to the wife of the new Parson at the Presbyterian Church. She was rather socially insecure as far as Preacher's wives go. He persuaded her that this garden would make her the envy of the church.

Charles was learning that one of the motives which drives purchases is often the "need" to be better than those around you. He had even sold a package to Ben Franklin himself. The old statesman had listened closely to his sales pitch and pronounced that it was a *Capital Idea!*

There were women who needed help designing their garden. And there were others who were jealous of Mrs. Culbertson's skills. All of them thought four shillings was a cheap price to learn her secrets. Spring planting time was already here.

Elizabeth had the charm of making Charles feel quite the hero. But she faced a new problem. He had sold all of the seed packets she had saved from the past year's garden, and now she was searching for a new product which would keep young Charles on his regular visits.

They decided on her apple butter as their next marketing venture. The young man was relieved to have a good reason for future visits. These brief visits with her always left him feeling so much better.

CHAPTER EIGHT
Perry's Stables

The short visit to see Elizabeth Culbertson had lifted his spirits.

As the Sun was falling low in the sky, Charles headed to where another informal council was being held. The next generation of pioneers tended to gather at the stable of Samuel Perry.

The stable was a good place for young men to pretend to be working. Mostly, this was a time for them to teach each other how to smoke, cuss, drink, and talk like "real men."

Bringing his friends up to speed on the news from the Gazette; Charles posed the question "Why wouldn't it work...just waiting for them to come across the pass and picking them off one at a time?"

Robert Cluggage (the oldest of the three Cluggage boys) offered the first criticism. "How long are we goanna have to sit on that pass to wait for them?"

Samuel Culbertson (Elizabeth's oldest brother) was next, "How are you gonna get food and water up on that mountain? And it gets mighty cold at night!"

"But that makes over 800!" Charles said in frustration.

"Eight hundred what?"

"Over 800 people have been killed or taken prisoner since this war started," young Cessna blurted out. "Somebody must do something. And they better do it soon!"

None of the others knew how to respond to his frustration. They understand where it had come from. His two brothers were still among the missing.

They did not know what to say. John Kirkpatrick Jr. was standing with the crowd. He was sorely feeling his own loss of a father and a brother. He had vivid memories of the killing he had witnessed.

Charles had been keeping mental a diary of every massacre and attack that he heard of. It was his mind's strange way of making sense of the chaos. Unlike most people in Pennsylvania he was beginning to get a picture of what was happening on the grander scale.

Although these young men were just a pack of friends conducting the rituals unique for each new generation of boys; this group was very special. They were the first generation born on this land. They would become the first generation of Americans. The future of these settlements rested on their courage and strength.

Their fathers looked on this war in a much different way. As immigrants they had purchased land from the Indians. They thought in terms of treating or purchasing peace from the natives as the solution to this war.

These young men had been born here, and viewed it as their right to live here. They were ready to fight to keep it. Most of them did not understand the sense of bribing the savages for peace.

And this group: the three Cluggage brothers, Widow Piper's two boys, three of the Adams boys, Samuel and James Culbertson, Tom Coulter, Robert Peebles, Samuel Perry, and the three oldest

Cessna boys were destined to become something else as well.

The hours spent in Perry's stables transformed them into a community. In a few short years they would carry this "community" about 70 miles down the wilderness trail. These boyhood friends would become the men who founded and built Bedford County.

That particular day though, they unanimously rejected Charles' idea as being too expensive and impractical. However, by engaging in the process of analyzing and evaluating the concept, they were forming themselves into a sort of "brain trust." They began to think of themselves as the solution to the future.

It was this generation (tempered by the experiences of a vicious Indian war) which formed the opinion that the red and white man could not live together. "The Indian must go!" was the sentiment expressed frequently. It soon felt like gospel for these young men.

The mere process of envisioning the future, bound them together for that future. They began to rely on each other's opinions and skills. There was no school in Shippensburg. Church meetings were sporadic. So this experience of gathering at Perry's Stable became their *alma mater*.

CHAPTER NINE
Pennsylvania Declares War

In the summer of 1758, Brigadier General John Forbes organized an army at Carlisle, 20 miles east of Shippensburg. He began a slow march on Fort Duquesne.

Like Braddock, he needed to build a dependable wagon road. It would permanently link the Three Rivers area to Philadelphia.

Unlike Braddock, he did not underestimate the Indians ability to make war. Every twenty-five miles, General Forbes built a sturdy fort to hold reinforcements and supplies. Wherever he could, he incorporated those locally built stockades previously inspired by Ben Franklin.

He spent tremendous amounts of money on moving men and materials ever closer to the enemy. By the time he approached Fort Duquesne, his strength was undeniable to the native allies of the French.

One by one, the Indian bands left their French allies and went home. When faced with unfavorable odds, the savages were civilized enough to choose not to fight.

As the English Army approached them, the French were alone and badly outnumbered. In the final days before the arrival of Forbes army, the fort was burned, and the French soldiers floated safely down the Ohio River.

While there continued to be isolated attacks on small groups of English Settlers, most of the war parties stopped coming over the mountains. Those warriors who were intent on continuing the fighting, now had to take their scalps and prisoners all the way to Fort Detroit to collect their rewards.

One detail which did not make the newspaper, but was passed up and down the valley by rumor, was a fact concerning their brilliant commander. During the entire campaign, General John Forbes had been terrible ill.

He had been carried by litter all the way from Carlisle to Fort Duquesne and back. Immediately after taking the French fort, he returned to Philadelphia. There he died on March 11, 1759.

Shippensburg was accustomed to seeing crowds of visitors. At times 500 pack animals and their drivers would fill the lanes of this tiny village. But nothing could have prepared the population for what happened in the summer of 1758.

Brigadier-General John Forbes arrived at Shippensburg with a force of regular army soldiers. Twelve hundred Scottish highlanders, complete with kilts and bagpipes, marched past the Cessna family store.

Most importantly, Forbes arrived with several chests full of English coin. If the army was going to be a shock on the enemy, its treasury was going to be an even greater shock on the Pennsylvania economy.

The army was buying up all of the surplus food and grain in Pennsylvania, Maryland, and Virginia. And it was hiring every spare horse, mule, oxen, and teamster within 100 miles of Carlisle.

The boys from Perry's Stables signed up almost to the man. John Cessna Jr. signed up as a teamster and brought eleven of the family's horses to serve in hauling freight.

Even Charles Cessna, who had little experience at driving pack animals signed up for the adventure. It was not his best skill, but Charles did not want to be left behind. He had two brothers out there somewhere, and he was determined to find them, if he could.

CHAPTER TEN
The Great Adventure of 1758

No one had ever seen so many men assembled in one place. For the most part, it was chaos, which served the mind of Charles quite well. He was able to see the confusion and quagmire from a distant vantage point, and spot opportunity when others were frustrated.

It seemed impossible to find anyone who really knew what was going on. There were lots of junior officers running around to give orders, but none of them seemed to agree as to what the teamsters should be doing.

Most days, the young men from Shippensburg just sat around waiting for someone to order them to "load those packs and head west."

Charles quickly figured out that the officers with the chests of cash were in control of the situation. They were buying everything they could and stockpiling it for the trip west. He attached himself to one lieutenant and began to learn what "supply" was all about.

Charles Cessna managed to get the job of loading and unloading the quartermaster's office and records each day. Charles watched closely as the officer followed his written orders to the letter.

He was assigned to buy certain quantity of hay, oats, and corn. When the farmers, arrived hoping to sell their surplus to the army, they were directed to his tent. He carefully recorded each purchase and with simple accounting skills, deducted it from the totals he had been directed to buy.

Young Cessna thought it curious that the officer regarded his accounting sheets as more valuable than the actual cash. But he gave both diligent and protective care.

Charles, had always thought in terms of buying a small quantity of this, and trading it for a small quantity of that. He was now introduced to government style purchasing. He was given lessons on the storing and care of such items as well. Each day he followed Lieutenant Jones on his inspection of the commodities already purchased. He must be sure they were being stored safely and wisely. He was also responsible for placing a guard over the army's resources.

It was far more complicated than young Cessna would have thought it could be. Being an eager student, Charles managed to secure some education in simple government accounting practices as well. He learned the vital importance of receipts....and paperwork.

After a delay of weeks, the Army was ready to move. The soldiers and weapons moved west at a slow crawl. They carved a new road out of the narrow bridle path that ran through the dense forest. The teamsters began a frantic scramble west and east, moving supplies down the road as it was created. Then they returned for another load.

Forbes planned to build a new wagon road from Carlisle out to Ft. Duquesne. His goal was the place where the Monongahela and Allegheny Rivers meet to form the mighty Ohio River. What had once been only an Indian and game path, would now be transformed into a level, all-weather wagon road.

For all practical terms, they were moving the threshold of civilization about two hundred miles further west. The western half of Pennsylvania would no longer be wilderness.

General Forbes was a careful planner. He intended to fight for this land only once. Every 20-30 miles he built a stockade and filled it with a surplus of the materials needed to fight the war. Each held hundreds of barrels of power, shot, clothes and food. Each had at least one canon.

Some of them would be merely storage depots. Others would be large fortresses which could provide protection for the populace. The stockades which had already been built at Shippensburg and Chambersburg were strengthened and filled to capacity with everything the Army might need. New forts were built at Littleton, Raystown, and Ligonier. Each was filled with enough supplies to last the army for months.

Charles was overwhelmed at so much in the way of stores. He estimated that General Forbes was having his officers purchase at least five times as much as would be needed.

The General was carefully placing duplicates of everything at strategic points along the road west. If he needed to retreat, he could stop at any one of these forts and outlast a significant siege. And if one or even two of the stockpiles were lost, he still had enough supplies to keep his army in the field for two years.

"An Army marches on its cooking pots!" proclaimed Lt. Jones. "And it is not any different for their livestock!"

"It looks to me that an Army marches on its paperwork" exclaimed Charles as he dropped a large wooden chest on the ground in front of the tent. Cessna and Thomas Jones had become attached to each other for the duration of this war.

Destined to become friends before this adventure ended, Charles had become a personal teamster for the Quartermaster officer. They had no way of knowing how their futures were fated to be closely intertwined.

As the Army moved through the wilderness, Lt. Jones was entrusted to oversee the safety of its supplies. He would personally supervise the construction of each storage building.

Charles Cessna was at the officer's side every step of the journey. Jones was tasked with inspecting the security precautions placed around the pack animals as they bedded down for each night's camp. It was Charles' job to shepherd the Lieutenant's portable office and files...and cash.

Now, the officer chuckled at Cessna's comment about the bulk of the paperwork. Charles used this moment to pose a question which had been troubling him all afternoon.

"I think I understand the difference between a *debit* and a *credit* but I am not sure what you mean that they have to balance each other."

The officer sat down to deliver another lecture about accounting. Charles continued to unpack the animals and set up the officer's desk as he talked.

Cessna had discovered that this was the best time to ply education from Lt. Thomas Jones. He did not much care for the sweaty labor of loading and unloading, so it was a suitable time to distract him with questions.

Jones enjoyed sitting on his chest of accounting books and money, while providing a lecture about logistics or bookkeeping. He talked and watched young Cessna do the work for both of them. Charles figured it was a small price to pay for the valuable education he was getting.

"It's not so difficult" continued Jones. "Income and Expenses; add and subtract! The balancing tells you if your numbers are right. Make a mistake with the King's money and you will pay the difference. Gotta keep the numbers in perfect balance."

Charles finished his labors and started an evening fire for both of them. Some nights he sought out his brothers and friends for their company. Other nights he would sleep near his supervisor and gain more information. Tonight would be one of the latter. He was in the mood for *schooling*.

John Cessna Sr. had provided a very basic education for the Cessna boys. In those early decades, there was no school in Shippensburg. Charles had been his most avid student, hungry for knowledge and the power it brought. His father had to borrow books from other Shippensburg men to keep ahead of the boy's appetite.

And when the Pennsylvania Gazette began to come to town on a regular basis, Charles devoured it like a starved hound. His knowledge of world politics, and his vocabulary grew with every issue of the newspaper. His ability to convey his thoughts was polished by the language he found there.

However, Father's knowledge of math was limited. Tonight, Charles hoped for another lesson from Lt. Thomas Jones. This one would address how to multiply and divide numbers greater than two digits.

Jones had the ability to figure out how much it would cost to feed an company of 100 soldiers for 120 days, when it cost 3 pence a day for rations. Charles intended to have that ability for himself.

Lt. Jones and his young aid were camped with a large stockpile of supplies just a few miles from Raystown. A new fort was being built there.

The stockade and its secure storage buildings were not finished. So the caravan of supplies was camped up and down the new road. Hundreds of men and horses stretched back over a mile in the direction of Shippensburg.

It seemed a hopeless mess to Charles. A fortune in material and food was stacked in small piles along the roadway wherever an open place in the forest was found. And the place they were taking it to, was little more than a wilderness itself.

About 1750, an Indian trader who people could barely remember, had built a trading post on a branch of the Juniata River. Though he lived here alone, travelers began to call it Raystown. By 1755, "Old Ray" had moved on to parts unknown and his home was nothing more than a ghostly legend. But the place was still called Raystown. You could look all day for a month and not find anything in the area that looked much like a town.

About the time Ray was leaving, Garrett Pendergrass moved in and opened a public house designed to wet the thirst of travelers. That is where Charles' brothers and friends would spend most of this particular evening.

Pendergrass was a mite addicted to drink and got very talkative when he was *in his cups*. His knowledge of the Indian and life in the woodlands was extensive. There was always a very entertaining evening waiting at Pendergrass' place.

The army began to build a new stockade and storage buildings near Pendergrass. Colonel Bouquet suggested they name the fort after the Duke of Bedford. The good Duke happened to be serving as the current Prime Minister of England. They thought it might garner a little favor from this politician.

They hoped he would send them a cannon or something expensive as a sign of appreciation. He was evidently unimpressed because he only sent them a lovely silk flag to fly over the stockade. Still, the fort and the community which grew around it would become known as Bedford.

The beauty and potential of this spot did not escape the boys from Shippensburg.

CHAPTER ELEVEN
The Scar

Almost all of the boys from the group attached to Perry's Stables would find a nice place to claim as their own in the mountain coves around Bedford.

Charles Cessna admired very much the piece of land he was standing on. The river at his back and the new highway at his front; what more could you ask. As near as he could tell, this road would be carrying lots of people, goods, and cash for years to come.

As the evening dew began to settle, the young man wrapped himself in a blanket and laid down by the fire. His dreams that night would be about the land around him, and a future life he might build here.

This place had lots of flat, open land to provide forage for the beasts which would be coming through here. As he drifted to sleep, his thoughts were focused on the possibility of building a home here, and perhaps a store.

Something heavy fell and knocked the wind out of him, startling him awake.

Charles was unable to move, and as the fog faded from his mind, he realized that he had been awakened by a rifle shot. Now he was being crushed with a heavy weight.

It was too much for him to piece together in the haze of sleep. Men were shouting and running towards him.

"Are you alive, son?" called a voice from the darkness. Two men began to roll something heavy off of him. He realized that it was a human body. Then the smell of it hit him. And he realized it was not any human he had been close to before. *It's an Indian! And he is dead on top of me!* The realization startled him to full alertness.

"What's going on?" demanded Lt. Jones.

Three men, who were obviously sentries, were standing around the body as a fourth man held a lantern to inspect it. It was not the first dead body that Charles had seen up close, but it was the most frightening.

"I seen me a shadow, just a creeping between that pile of baggage and your tent." One of the men reported.

"Wasn't sure just what it was, till I saw a glimmer off of some kind of metal. Figured whoever it was, wasn't up to no good with that boy there, so I shot him."

Charles was sitting up by now, though still badly shaken. For the first time he realized that by sleeping near the fire, he had made a visible target of himself. This point was driven home by an exceptionally long scalping knife that lay in the grass near him. His stomach dropped suddenly as his mind recognized his narrow escape with death.

"You are bleeding," said Jones. "Come to my tent and let me see how bad it is."

Blood was running down the right side of his face, and as his fingers searched out its source, he realized he had a deep cut in his hair line.

The knife had found a mark as the Indian fell on him. Instantly fear filled him. He had not been afraid until he saw the blood on his fingers.

But now, he was so seized by it that he could not make his legs work. Two of the men grabbed him to his feet and pulled him into Jones' tent.

The rest of the night was a blur. He was vaguely aware of having the wound cleaned, bandaged, and eventually bedding down again. This time on the floor of Lt. Jones' tent.

Charles slept until the sun was high enough to make the tent overly warm. He sat up to be greeted by a terrible headache. It had all seemed like a bad dream.

War and fighting were not supposed to sneak up on you in your sleep. But the news of the morning was that no less than six other incursions had happened up and down the lines over night.

Some of the braves had managed to steal horses and supplies. One or two had been scared off by the sentries. Only Charles' attacker had been determined to collect a scalp. Everyone would be on high alert from that night on.

Charles Cessna was invited to sleep inside the supply officer's tent from that day until the expedition ended. In his entire life, this would be the closest that Charles Cessna would ever come to dying in a war. And the scar on his hairline would make a wonderfully impressive trophy to show in public settings.

Though there were no heroics involved on his part of the incident, it had given him a heroic air.

The quartermaster corps spent the rest of the year moving men and supplies up and down the road from Carlisle. With every trip, Charles discovered that the wilderness had been pushed back another 20 miles or so.

Lt. Jones had the duty of returning to Carlisle or Shippensburg and buying the next massive load of food, clothes, and whatever. Then he was responsible for forming a convoy of freighters to carry all of it to the newest fort being built. With that done, he returned to start the process over again. He was in constant travel up and down the new road. Charles Cessna was with him.

Each of the forts became so well stocked they were like small cities. Many of the teamsters were already claiming the most prize pieces of farmland around these forts. A town would grow around each one. It was not hard to see that more land was being settled with each of their excursions.

Charles Cessna's older brother, John, was one of those men who were talking about taking up some of the new land. He had his eye set on a narrow valley leading from Fort Bedford to Fort Cumberland in Maryland.

By the end of 1758, General Forbes had completed his mission. The French had abandoned Fort Duquesne. And the English army had moved the British Empire all the way to the Ohio River. Farms and trading posts began to appear along the edges of the road which was now called Forbe's Road.

The war between France and England continued on other fronts around the globe. But only occasional war parties came skulking through the passes into Cumberland Valley.

Life in Shippensburg returned to normal. Crops were planted and harvested without interruption.

Guns were kept close, but fear visited less often. Young men began to think of taking wives and clearing new land.

Charles began to sense the peace he had so needed in his life. He felt he had important things to do with his life, but the war kept getting in his way.

CHAPTER TWELVE
My Land

"**W**hy not? I deserve an answer!"

"The answer is **NO!**"

Charles Cessna had slipped in the back entrance to Perry's Stables. He could hear the heated confrontation as he entered. But he was surprised to see who the combatants were.

Confrontations among young men were nothing rare in this haven of manhood. And this warm day in June of 1762 seemed as good a day as any to start a ruckus.

Charles was surprised at the combatants. Sam Culbertson, noted for his calm nature, had never been included in one of these contests. Now Sam had been backed against a wall by an overly emotional Thomas Coulter. Tom was demanding a satisfactory answer. Sam was not one to be pushed beyond his boundaries. It appeared that a really good, lip-splitting conclusion was about to occur.

Other members of the group were moving to separate them. Coulter offered the group a fresh lesson in profane exclamations, and stormed out of the far end of the stables.

The Piper boys had been hanging back to avoid the fray. Each of them had tangled with Coulter before and did not desire a renewal of the experience.

"What are the *confustications?*" asked Charles of the Piper boys. He was trying out a new word he had recently discovered in the Gazette. He had been feeling in a particularly good mood when he entered the barn. That would quickly change.

"Lizzie!"

"Who?" pursued Charles.

"Sam has a little sister, Lizzie. Tom has been asking for permission to come courting, but Sam won't budge on the issue. And he won't give Tom a good reason either. If you ask me, Tom is hurting his case by getting so worked up. But it ain't none of my affair."

Young Cessna was caught short by the news. Until that very moment, he had not even considered that Elizabeth Culbertson was old enough to court. He certainly had not considered that there might be a competition for her.

Cautiously, he began to probe the other young men for details about the scene he had just missed. He realized that he had missed a lot of the drama surrounding his pretty young friend. Charles began to apprise her as being much more desirable than he had earlier.

Elizabeth is old enough to court? And there are other men considering her? Where has your mind been, boy? How could you miss something so obvious? What if she likes Tom Coulter more than you?

I guess I had better make my mind up. Maybe I should tell her how I feel. How do I feel?

He was trying to remember the color of Elizabeth's eyes when he was called back to the present. James Cessna, his youngest brother, came running into the barn.

"Charles, ma says to come straight home. You got a caller!"

Immediately, the young men in the barn began to give the child a tough time. He was too young to be in the presence of their secret conclave. Charles stepped in to rescue his sibling.

To say that James' news was a shock, is an understatement. Charles had never had anyone come to the house asking specifically for him. Together, they hurried back to the Cessna Tavern.

"Thom?" Charles exclaimed, when he saw his old friend on the porch, talking with his father. The last time Charles had seen his friend, Lt. Jones had been marching with the Army back to Philadelphia. They each had assumed that their goodbye was the last time they would see each other again.

The reunion was a happy one. Thom Jones was impressed with how much his assistant had matured in two years' time. He was also impressed with how much Charles Cessna's sister, Elizabeth, had matured in that time. She was hiding coyly, just out of sight behind the door jam. She leapt back in embarrassment as Charles caught sight of her.

The young men hugged in pure brotherly joy and immediately began to exchange jibes of mock derision. Their friendship was honest and deep. John Cessna Sr. was delighted to see the boys in such a good mood. He was already taking a liking to his son's friend.

"What are you doing back here?" Charles asked. "You haven't deserted the Army are you?"

Thom Jones laughed. "Not in this life! My enlistment was up. And when I was passed over for Captain I decided to try this lazy life you civilians have. I have had enough of counting socks and buckles."

"But you had planned to go home to take care of your mum?"

"Mum died in December. I guess there is really no one to go back to England for." Thom's grief was obvious, and Charles decided to push that subject no further. He knew that nearly all of his friend's army pay had gone home to support his mother.

"Well then my friend, you have come to the right place." Charles took a deep breath as though he were about to make a profound statement. "But no one out here has more than two pair of socks and one buckle to go around. So counting them has never been hard." Both men laughed.

"I guess I need to find a new career then!" announced Thom. What followed was three hours of drinking, laughing, and suggestions of improbable careers for this ex-soldier who had spent the entire war counting things.

In the days ahead, Jones was easily absorbed into the community of young men in Shippensburg. The former officer was welcomed into the Cessna family as well. He quickly earned the appreciation of everyone.

Young Elizabeth Cessna was obviously, although shyly, an avid admirer. Frequently she was found standing where she would not be seen, but could hear every word that Mr. Jones said.

The second generation of pioneers began to realize that their futures did not lie in Shippensburg. All of the good land had been purchased by their fathers. When the patriarch died, the oldest son would inherit the estate, and the others would have to go into the wilderness and carve their own fortunes.

So the young men of Charles Cessna's age were looking in the only direction available to them... WEST! Charles Cessna thought it strangely predictable how the destruction of War always heralds a frantic period of construction.

John Cessna Sr. had been expecting and predicting this as well, and had been frantically collecting every coin that he could throughout the war. The Cessna family was ready for what would come next.

In the Fall of 1759, John Cessna Jr., and Sarah started a new homestead 70 miles west of Shippensburg. John chose a place about 15 miles south of Fort Bedford. It came with the name "The Block Houses" because in the recent past someone had built fortifications on either side of Evitts Creek. People who were under siege were able to cover each other from the dual forts.

The army still had lots of private freighters bringing supplies up from Fort Cumberland. In fact, the spot on the road John chose was at the midpoint of the two day trip between these two forts. It was a favorite place for the teamsters to spend the night.

John and Sarah Cessna built a cabin large enough to serve as a tavern/way station. Together, they were repeating what John Cessna, Sr. had done in Shippensburg, 20 years earlier.

The land office in Carlisle reopened.

The excitement was palpable among the group of men in Perry's Stables. Young men began to dream of prosperous futures. Land was available!

The process of settlement began again. For a small amount of cash, men could buy warrants to land in the west. It was then their right to wander into the wilderness, and select a piece of ground for their future home.

They would claim it and pay quit rents while they made "improvements." After a couple years of building, and hopefully profitable harvests, they could apply for a patent. For another fee, the government would officially survey the claim and issue final title.

John Cessna Sr. had been waiting for this moment...and was prepared. Calling his sons together he presented both Charles and Evans with a small sack of coins. Each contained enough to purchase a warrant to settle 200 acres in the western lands. It was like opening the gate for a pack of young stallions.

Similar scenes were happening between fathers and sons all around Shippensburg. In June of 1762, a new army formed in the street outside the stone house of John Cessna Sr.

It was the Perry's Stables group, forming an expedition to seek out land in the area around Bedford. They had chosen to go as a group for safety. Each held a piece of paper from the land office. It gave them permission to claim as much land as they could afford.

The group spent two weeks exploring the coves around Fort Bedford, marking out their claims. From 1762-66, every one of the young men from the Perry's stables group would choose land around Bedford as his personal future.

The area around the fort became densely settled. Among those Shippensburg men who settled there were Elisha Adams, Robert Adams, Anthony Adams, John Montgomery, William McCall, and Robert Peebles.

Boys who once played the dusty streets of Shippensburg, now became the community leaders and creators of what was quickly becoming Bedford County.

Many of the group were attracted to the area where John Cessna Jr. had started his place. With his encouragement, the land around him quickly filled up.

Robert Hall and Evans Cessna, married each other's sister (Margaret Cessna and Mary Hall). The two friends partnered in a 300 acre land grant.

Thom Jones was not to be left behind. Elizabeth Cessna had openly declared her intentions for him. In a series of negotiations with her father, Lt. Jones was given enough money to start a farm as well.

Ever the wise investor, John Cessna Sr. insisted that the land be titled to both Thomas Jones and Charles Cessna, in partnership. Charles had already decided to set his own house near to that of Jones anyway, so the partnership idea was welcome.

Charles and Evans Cessna laid out claims along Evitts Creek. They were about 3 miles from the home of John and Sarah Cessna, and about 13 miles south of Fort Bedford.

Strength lay in numbers and this group of friends began to form a neighborhood of farms which would later become known as Centerville. Its name came from the fact that it lay about halfway through the journey from Fort Bedford to Fort Cumberland.

Evitts Creek provided a year round supply of spring fed water. The high ridges on either side of this narrow valley provided a snug break from storms.

When the group returned to Shippensburg, Charles Cessna was more than excited. He could hardly wait to see Elizabeth Culbertson and tell her about his plans.

It was now quite an effort to see Elizabeth.

After the war, her family moved back to their farm on Culbertson's Row. She no longer lived just down the street from him. It was a good 7 miles from town. But the farm gave them more opportunities for privacy.

CHAPTER THIRTEEN
The Way of A Man And A Woman

Charles Cessna, owned a farm! It was wilderness land. It had only the nucleus of a farm on it. But it was a place he could build.

He began to dream for the future.

Elizabeth Culbertson was now fully blossomed at 17 years. Their partnership had grown so much that he was totally dependent upon her approval for every choice he made.

The way she said "Mr. Cessna" had become something of an addiction for him. Her affirmation was intoxicating. He needed to experience it as often as possible.

Pulling her to a private place in the farmyard, he told her of his fortune. He described this new land so rapidly that she could not find a pause to squeeze a word in.

Elizabeth let the young man talk his heart out. As he spoke, her own mind was racing with the possibilities before them. When he paused to catch his breath, she reached out and took his hand in hers.

With an affirming squeeze she told him of her great approval of his news. That was all it took. She need not say a word. Her eyes, her smile, the grip of her hand on his, all of it told him what he needed to hear.

Charles immediately stopped talking. He took her in his arms and kissed her passionately. It was their first real kiss. It was *the kiss*.

It united them more certainly than any proposal and engagement. Instantly they both knew that their futures were bound together. That future was waiting on this land he was describing.

Holding her in his arms, with his face buried in her neck, a new sensation came over him. He had never felt it before. He could not find a word to describe it.

Charles and Elizabeth held each other for a long time, exchanging kisses. It was as though their partnership of three years had been storing up a plethora of passion. Now, with the door open, it all came flooding out.

Another door opened moments later. Mrs. Culbertson came out of her cabin calling her daughter. She had spied the long anticipated event. And she had given the young people about as much time as she dared before interrupting them.

Red-faced, Charles Cessna made a hasty retreat towards home. They did not see each other for three days. But during that time, each was rehearsing in their mind what would come next in their lives.

Each dreamed of building a cabin; planting a farm and garden; and falling into each other's arms at night. They had become such efficient partners, that the plans each made separately, were remarkably similar to those of the other.

"We have to talk," Elizabeth whispered to him at Church on Sunday. "Come to the big Cottonwood at dusk."

Ignoring the danger from Indians, or being caught by their parents, Charles came. He was haunted by the feeling of having his face buried in the crook of her neck. He desperately wanted to understand it.

Beneath a half moon hanging low in the Eastern sky, and a canopy of stars, they began to talk and share visions. The hopes of each seemed a perfect fit for the other.

Charles was entranced with how perfectly it all seemed to be coming together. He was already naming their children. And she was agreeing with every suggestion.

They were talking in terms of decades not days or weeks. When they got tired of conversation, she kissed him again. All talking stopped as each began to taste the life in the other. The comfort of this embrace was completely disarming.

There is that feeling again, he thought. It completely captured Charles' attention as he inhaled the smell of her hair and skin. He nuzzled behind her ear.

There it is again! Suddenly the feeling had a name. Standing here, with this girl in his arms, his face buried in her neck, smelling, and tasting her...he felt... *at home!*

It felt like he should have been there all his life...and should be in that warm place for the rest of his life. He suddenly knew that his future would be found in this young slip of a girl.

Everything felt sure and right. She belonged in his arms. Anything in them which might have been a child, vanished that night. They became a man and a woman.

Solomon, in all his wisdom, said he could not begin to understand the magical way of a man with a woman. Charles and Elizabeth were no wiser in comprehending or controlling what was happening to them. Passion overpowered them.

Hours later, they walked back to her cabin. They were certain of the future, and convinced of their love. Charles Cessna had never felt more victorious in his entire life. There were no doubts. Everything was clear to him.

He finally fell asleep in the early hours of morning; with the most confident feeling he had ever known.

He woke to the deepest feelings of shame, and self-condemnation he had ever known.

What have I done? What if she hates me for this? Did I ruin her life? What if her mother guesses what I've done? Elizabeth might end up hating me for this. I can't lose her. What should I do? She will be ruined if anyone finds out what happened. What if she... has a BABY?"

Overcome with the guilt of what he had done, he began to blame himself for having taken advantage of the girl. It was his fault!

Charles knew what had to be done. They would marry. They would do so right now!

He just had to find a way to convince his father, and her brother, and his mother, and her mother. And he needed a way to convince Elizabeth.

Charles felt so unworthy of her that he did not know how he would ever face her again. He considered many different options, most of them involved running away in shame. A 21 year old man, blinded by passion AND love, can have a tough time responding in moderation.

Finally, he knew what he must do. Though he had no home to bring her to, nor much money, she had to marry him! It was the "right" thing to do, and he would not be dissuaded from it.

"Father?" Charles said with courageous effort to sound as mature as possible. "May I speak with you."

John Cessna Sr. was taken aback by the boy's attitude. His tone meant they were to have a conversation as equals, and John was not ready for such a thing. In his late 50's, John was not really on an intimate relationship with the children of his second marriage.

John Jr, the son of his first marriage, was the only child with whom he had bonded. They had been reluctant partners for over 30 years.

His relationship with the other children was more like that of a school master, or employer. So when Charles approached him with a desire to speak as equals he was unprepared.

"Father, I think I am ready to marry." Charles announced with a deliberate effort to sound confident and mature. His voice cracked a bit at the word "marry" and his face reddened.

Hesitating only a brief moment, his father bellowed "Nonsense!". "You can't even take care of yourself yet! How can you possibly take care of a wife?

"Where would the two of you live? Do you plan on keeping her in the loft with your brothers?" John threw his hands in a motion that clearly ended the conversation. But Charles persisted.

"I have some money," insisted Charles. "And I have land in Cumberland Valley Township. It is enough to get started."

"Ha! You haven't cut the first tree or ploughed the first row on that land. And most of the time you are hanging around here letting me feed you! You ain't ready! Probably won't be ready for another ten years!"

As Charles face grew red in anger, his shame deepened. His father stormed out of the room. Charles was left with no hope of continuing this conversation.

His father's words were true. Most men didn't marry until they were in their late 20's. They needed to have a home and prosperous farm to take the bride to. You needed a good amount of cash to impress a girl's father (or in his case her brothers). Charles had nothing but dreams and possibilities.

In that moment he almost gave up the entire idea. It was impossible to marry Elizabeth Culbertson. But the memory of her eyes, the smell of her neck, and the way she said "Mr. Cessna" drove his mind to pursue the dream.

Yes, I am young, but 21 is not a boy. Yes, I have a little money. And I have more ways to make money than most people do. I have to find a way!

What if she is pregnant? What if Tom Coulter finally convinces her brothers? I have to find a way to make it happen right now!

In great despair he confessed his dilemma to his older brother. John was now a married man with a son, and a farm. John Cessna Jr. had been expecting the partnership of Charles and Elizabeth to blossom into something more. But he was surprised with how quickly it had all happened.

John almost sided with their father. But something in him sensed what was driving Charles' urgency in this issue. A few direct questions told John the true nature of their problem. He pulled Charles to a meeting with Elizabeth's oldest brother.

Samuel Culbertson was also improving a farmstead just a few miles from Bedford. His new farm was only 1 mile from that of John Cessna.

Though he expected to get punched for it, Charles confessed his failings. And he professed his complete love for the girl.

Sam Culbertson must have been touched by his performance. Together, the two older brothers struck a deal that would save the couple from possible disgrace. The older men would escort the couple to Bedford. The Presbyterian minister was making his circuit and would be in Chambersburg. It was on the way.

The older brothers would vouch for the couple. Because her father was dead, Samuel would offer his permission for Elizabeth to marry. John Cessna, Jr. would vouch that Charles was twenty-one.

Charles and Elizabeth would leave Shippensburg single, but arrive in Bedford married. They would live with John Jr. while their own home was being built.

Charles hoped that by the time a baby was born, only a few busybodies would be the wiser. Such things were not given much attention on the frontier.

It was a awkward and comical scene when the three determined men arrived at the Culbertson home. In embarrassed terms they explained the scheme to Elizabeth. Appalled at the lack of romance, she started to tell them all to go to the devil.

Then she decided that it fit nicely into her own plans. With a hurried pack, and a hasty goodbye, the four were off to a new life.

The Widow Culbertson was speechless. She remained that way till the group was out of sight. But the younger children said she did not stop ranting about the event for three more days.

Mr. and Mrs. Cessna began their married life with everything borrowed. They had nothing. Still they made a perfect partnership.

Each worked feverously to gather the things needed, and build a home for their life together. They may have started behind and without; but they had no intention of staying that way for long.

Elizabeth actually considered herself fortunate for the turn of events. Usually, a man built his home and farm the way he wanted it. The bride was carried to a home that had been designed and built by a man. Elizabeth now had the chance to plan her life from the beginning.

Mrs. Cessna chose the spot on their property where the house should sit. She picked the direction it would face. She decided the distance from the house to place the well.

Elizabeth designed the outhouse, and the smokehouse, and the chicken house, and the stables, and the woodpile. She conceived a house that was a larger than usual size log home. It was built in a U- shape.

Along the north wall was a large room about 30 x 20 feet with a huge fireplace. From each end, a 10 x 10 room was extended to the south, with a covered porch between them.

It was much bigger than Charles would have built had he planned it. Over the two rooms were built sleeping lofts "for the children." One room was their bedroom. The other she declared was to be Mr. Cessna's office.

Elizabeth was absolutely convinced that her husband was going to be a gentleman of consequence in the community. And she insisted that their home be worthy of the man he was to become. Though he had never thought of public life, Charles was touched by her insistence that he was going to be important someday.

Anxious for privacy, they moved into the house as soon as walls and roof were complete. But the baby did not come as he expected. Charles had yet to learn that it often takes more than one coupling to create a life. Elizabeth had not got pregnant from that one night as he had feared.

She did, however, manage to conceive during the first few weeks after their wedding. Charles Cessna Jr. was born to them in 1763. He would soon be joined by brothers, John and Samuel.

Those sons were named for the two older brothers who had "rescued" the young couple from embarrassment.

CHAPTER FOURTEEN
Fatherhood

Charles Jr. was destined to be a troublesome character in his father's life. He was not a fussy baby. He was not given to the fits of accusatory crying which most babies use to manipulate their parents.

Even as an infant, Charles had the ability to make his father uncomfortable. He simply sat quietly and stared with silent questions in his eyes.

Whether the questions that Charles Cessna felt his son was asking of him were real, or from his own imagination, did not really matter. Charles would frequently find the boy just studying him with wide eyes. The boy was probably only curious, but the young father's conscience began to imagine soul searching questions in the boy's eyes.

Charles might enthusiastically be recounting some adventure, opportunity, or political argument with his bride; and suddenly be caught up short by the look in his son's eyes. The boy said nothing. But Charles was continually stopped in his discourse by something he saw in the boy's eyes.

Without realizing it, Charles became dependent on his son's opinions...long before the boy was able to speak his first word.

Though among the youngest of the couples in the area, Charles and Elizabeth Cessna were certainly the most enthusiastic about building community. Elizabeth and a few friends organized weekly markets in the field outside Fort Bedford.

On Saturdays, dozens of families would gather to swap produce, wild teas, scraps of cloth, handmade tools, and other resources. Women held councils about how the community should grow. They kept tabs on who was pregnant. The men used the time to *confer on important matters*. And the children used the time to test themselves against each other.

Saturday Markets were the central entertainment for the hard working frontier families. If this happened to be the week when the preacher was in town, Cessnas just camped overnight for Sunday meeting.

Charles was always impressed with the load of goods his wife had managed to gather for each week's market. Her kitchen garden was abundant to say the least. And he was even more impressed with the many things she brought home in triumph. He continued to blush when she called him Mr. Cessna in front of his friends. But he felt truly lucky.

In October of 1762, three young boys presented themselves at the gate of Fort Detroit and asked to be returned to their families. They had been adopted into the Ottawa People and claimed to have been held captive for five years.

Though they looked like savages, the boys claimed to be Joseph (15) and Jonathan (12), sons of John Cisney; and Joseph Kirpatrick (12), son of the Widow Kirkpatrick.

Col. Burd, the commander at Detroit happened to be from Shippensburg and recognized their story.

All three boys arrived home in January. Agnes Cessna was beyond ecstatic with the completion of her prophecy.

John Sr. immediately bought more land in Cumberland Valley Township near the farmsteads being taken up by his other sons. It was placed in the names of Joseph (only 15) and Jonathan (only 12).

The brothers lost to the Indians were going to be Charles' neighbors. Life seemed to be finally taking a turn toward prosperity. Charles Cessna beamed with pride as he introduced his family to the lost brothers.

But these prodigal sons brought news with them of a new Indian War. An Ottawa Chief named Pontiac was sending wave after wave of war parties into their valleys. Within months, Fort Bedford was under siege and isolated farmers were being murdered.

Once again, the settlers of Bedford were forced to withdraw their families to the safety of Shippensburg. New stories of murdered families and travelers, came each week.

Charles began to berate his young and foolish behavior. He had a wife and son. A second child was on the way. His home was not finished. He did not have even half of the equipment needed to start a farm. Now he had to abandon everything to take his family to safety.

His father had been right, he was far too young and unprepared to start a family. He had been determined to prove the doubters wrong. If he had to work harder, he would. Whatever it took, he was going to make this work. Now with a new threat of Indian raids, he had a hard choice to make.

Moving quickly among the neighbors in Centerville he convinced them that they were not ready to mount a defense. An impromptu wagon train was organized to carry the refugees back to the safety of Shippensburg.

It took two nights and three days of rushed travel to reach safety. Each of those nights his young wife cried herself to sleep in his arms. Each of those nights he lay awake, berating himself for not protecting his family better.

He had eloped from Shippensburg ahead of any public criticism. Now he was crawling back with his pregnant wife and son. And he had no way to care for them. He would have to ask for his father's help. His father would not be gracious about giving it.

Charles Cessna realized he was now one of those pitiful refugees that had filled his town in the last war. It was impossible for him to admit his shame. He had to do something! Charles Cessna was a different man in this war.

He had spent several nights with a tearful and pregnant wife in his arms. Elizabeth had lost her father in the last Indian war. She now feared she might also lose her husband.

Charles Cessna was not about to let his fate be shuffled by the winds of war. Nor was he a hot headed young man ready to grab a rifle and head out for vengeance. He was determined to do something about this conflict. His mind sought options to make changes in their situation.

Remembering the lessons of the last war, he felt they could not wait for the government to mount an army. Too many lives would be lost.

Charles began to pressure the men of Bedford and Shippensburg to raise their own militia and take the fight to the Indians. He found a strong ally in a young man named James Smith.

Smith had been a captive of the Indians during the last war. He understood their methods of fighting. He bragged that an elite group of trained fighters could do much to intercept their murderous raids.

But it took money and support to operate such a group. Charles knew it would be impossible to convince anyone in government of this tactic.

Through emotional and persuasive arguing, Charles Cessna convinced the Committee of Public Opinion that direct action was needed. When the issue of funding was raised, Charles had a quick remedy.

Following the example set by Ben Franklin in the 1740's, Charles Cessna organized a lottery. Enough money was raised in two weeks to keep a company of men in the field for four months.

James Smith was made its captain and he trained a select group to respond to Indian incursions. His men dressed in the clothing and weaponry of the Indians. There were a number of former child-captives who volunteered in this company of rangers.

They made frequent patrols through the woods in front of the settlements. They provided a protective escort to bring isolated farm families into the forts. They fought several significant skirmishes with the invaders, and saved many lives. The experiment convinced Charles that an organized effort was needed to curb the power of their enemy.

Charles Cessna had strong suspicions that this was not going to be the last war with the red man.

Elizabeth Cessna looked at her husband through heroic eyes. She had watched his efforts to protect their community. Though few gave recognition to it, she knew that it had been his vision and efforts to form the ranging militia. That had made the difference.

She wondered how many women and children were alive because he had persisted with the lottery and Captain Smith's rangers. He did not get community recognition, but he was heralded in his home.

This time it was Colonel Bouquet who led the army which marched back to the forks of the Ohio and forced the invaders to stop.

Peace followed in a few months.

CHAPTER FIFTEEN
Giving Birth to a Community

"**T**hat is the most worthless idea I ever heard of" said Tom Coulter in a near shout. "*Mr. Cessna,* seems to have lost his mind."

He had never spoken directly to Charles Cessna about his rejection for Elizabeth's hand by the Culbertson family. But Tom never missed a chance to challenge Charles in any public debate.

Coulter could never like the man who had stolen the girl of his dreams. It was a prickly point for each of the men, that their farms were next to each other. It was not hard for each to see the other's happiness (or lack of it) from their own front porch.

And Coulter continued to flirt with Elizabeth Cessna whenever an opportunity presented itself. Coulter had taken a habit of saying *Mr. Cessna* with great sarcasm whenever they spoke. Charles understood it as a dig at the affectionate way Elizabeth used the phrase to make her husband feel heroic. Tom used it to make him feel small.

Coulter loved to engage Cessna in debate. And public debate was becoming a weekly exercise for the new settlers of Bedford. Coulter and Cessna were often found opposing each other over one issue after another.

Following the war, the families returned to their land claims. Each began working hard to improve their estate, earn money from surplus crops, and get a good start on their families.

By 1769, many of the more successful men had reached a place where they could turn their energies towards building a stronger community. The years of peace had seen these young men grow to maturity and prosperity. The stockade at Fort Bedford slipped silently into neglect and decay, even as the quality of homes and sophistication of their farms increased.

Bedford was becoming quite a nice little town. And so was born the tumult of small town politics.

Charles Cessna, Bernard Dougherty, and a number of men gravitated towards keeping decision making on the local level as much as possible. This meant that in order to lead, one had to make a lot of friends, and demonstrate a good deal of common sense.

Tom Coulter, George Woods, and others were more inclined to appeal to the Governor and Proprietaries (Penn Family) for as many decisions as possible. This meant that political appointments would come from Philadelphia. A person did not have to be popular with your neighbors to be given authority over them. It might be a total stranger who was appointed.

The English system of patronage was well established. And as far as some were concerned, it was the most efficient way to get things done. Patronage and bribery were the ways person rose to political power in the King's government.

Charles Cessna had been debating with the men at Pendergrass' Inn about petitioning for

Bedford to be declared a new county. He was of the strong opinion that they should hold their own elections and send the results to the Governor for his acceptance.

Coulter felt that this was brash and would only irritate the governor. He was in favor of a petition asking the Governor to consider organizing a new county for them. While the outward results might be the same, the chain of power created by each method was substantially different.

"If we let the governor choose, we won't have any say in who is appointed as judge, or sheriff, or tax collector." Charles insisted.

"They might just send some silk shirted dandy from England in here to tell us how to live. How can it hurt to tell the governor who among us we think would make a good officer?"

"*Mr. Cessna* would have us insult the governor by telling him we know how to govern better than he. That is certain to win us lots of friends in Philadelphia" Coulter retorted.

And with that, the debate was in full swing. Soon accusations were made about who was making a grab for power. Cessna was attacked because he had a lot of brothers and friends in the area, and people felt certain he would be elected to offices of power. Coulter and Woods were accused of having insider friends in Philadelphia who would give them the power.

Charles had seen it happen so many times before. Every time he suggested the community act together to improve itself, he was accused of being grandiose, and seeking power. Yet all of his suggestions had been for the community's good, not his alone.

He had pushed for the farmers to form a loose cooperative in marketing their surplus grain. He had pushed for some rules about using Evitts Creek so that those living downstream had the benefit of clean water.

Charles had even mentioned the need for some kind of a militia organization, but in the absence of war no one wanted to spend time or money in that direction. Without realizing what was happening, Charles was embracing a new philosophy of politics. Until his generation, government officials were all *Servants of the King.*

But slowly the idea emerged that these officials should be *Public Servants.* It was a simple but profound shift of ideology.

In the end, the traditionalists won out. The men of the community made a petition for the governor to form a new county. They argued that the chance of success was greater if they appealed to his ego to make the choices for them.

The Governor sent strangers to be the Sheriff, Judge, and County Clerk. This did move the benefits of government closer to them. No longer would they have to appeal all the way to Carlisle for help from a Sheriff or Justice of the Peace.

Their own first elections of county officers were held in December of 1771. The two candidates for each office who had the most votes were referred to the governor. The governor and council would then choose one of these two to serve in office. Or they might choose someone else altogether; the lazy nephew of someone who made a large bribe, for example. It was an interesting split of power.

In April of 1771, John Cessna and his brother Charles were members of the first Grand

Jury for the new county of Bedford. For the next dozen years, John and Charles would serve their community in a number of public offices. John would serve as Juror, Sheriff, Tax Collector, representative to Provencial Council and eventually Justice of the Peace.

Charles would serve as Juror, County Commissioner, County Purchaser, and Representative to the State Assembly. Their brothers, Evans and Jonathan, each took a turn serving as constable.

It is an old adage that the cream rises to the top. It is also a true fact that in the frontier communities, men who work hard and have a long range vision rise to the top of political power. Some were using that power to promote their own interests. Others used their prophetic visions to build a better community.

Every indication is that Charles and John Cessna were men of the later persuasion. Each took his turn in serving. Several times, when they lost an election, the Cessna brothers would offer bond in support of the neighbor they had just lost the election to.

This is not to say that they were not involved in the upheaval of political discussion. In January of 1775, Charles was on a jury that tried to settle a dispute of some notoriety.

The court's decision was to charge, on behalf of the King, Mr. Edward Higgins, to keep peaceful for one year on penalty of 100 pounds sterling if he failed. And in the same incident, Charles voted to order Thomas Jones and John

Cessna to keep the peace for one year, especially towards Daniel Stoy, on penalty of 50 pounds sterling each if they failed. He had no leniency for his brother and brother-in-law.

Charles Cessna was quite pleased with his little community. Peace and prosperity were the order of the day. The only strife came from political debate and shenanigans, and there was no escaping that.

But taxes were being paid. Public monies were staying here in the county to make improvements. Crime was being punished more swiftly, and by a jury of one's neighbors. Property disputes were being settled quickly and roads were being constructed.

Civilization was moving along quite nicely. And occasionally, Charles got to see public issues work out the way he wanted them to.

One of his "victories" came on the issue of taxes. Cash money could be scarce at times in the western communities. If you did not have cash to pay your taxes, the court could seize your farm and the Sheriff would sell it at auction.

Charles was able to convince the Commissioners that some farmers should be allowed to pay their taxes with surplus crops. Unable to quickly convert flour and corn meal into cash, Cessna suggested storing it against a future emergency or need.

Cessna managed to design and construct a storehouse for grain, leather, and other supplies. While technically it all belonged to the King and the Penn Family; it stood ready to provide relief in their county if it was needed.

Charles had become a public figure. He was well known and respected, although a sizable number of people disagreed with his views. Charles Cessna was called away from home more often. He needed to participate in some debate or political episode.

Mr. Cessna was a frequent visitor in Bedford, although it was a half day's ride from his farm. His farm was being neglected by his absence. At the suggestion of his wife, Charles purchased his first slave.

Rubicon, was employed with the day to day operations of the farm. This left Charles more time to participate in his "community building activities."[1] His in-laws, the Culbertsons, were supporters of using slave or indentured labor to hasten one's pursuit of wealth.

"Rube" did enable Charles to prosper and also become a public personage. But it alienated him from his brothers and a good number of friends. Most free men were not happy to see slave labor enter the marketplace of their community. Slaves would do most anything cheaper than the honest wages a craftsmen needed.

---

[1] The true name given this slave is unknown.

CHAPTER SIXTEEN
1775

"It just don't make sense!" cried Tom Coulter. And behind him a room full of men broke out in loud murmurings.

Nearly 50 men had gathered at the tavern of John Bonnet that spring evening. They had come to hear the report of William Thompson who had just returned from Philadelphia.

"It does make sense," asserted Thompson, "if you consider how much Parliament has been laying new taxes on the Americas. There is no one in London to represent us, so those corrupt politicians just make up any law and tax they want. We have a right to our own congress, and to make the laws we need."

William Thompson was quite red-faced by this point in the argument. He had not expected this much contention. He had forgotten that Coulter and a few others had strong opinions and fully believed that their neighbors were delighted to hear them.

Coulter was not happy to hear that the colonies had decided to set up their own parliament... or Continental Congress ...or whatever they wanted to call it.

"We have been seeing lots of stories in the *Gazette*, about a move afoot to bring our government closer to us," remarked Charles Cessna. "I for one don't see how that can be a bad thing."

"Well, the governor of Virginia thought it was a bad thing. He dissolved their legislature and declared martial law." This came from Bernard Dougherty. He was another community leader who followed closely what was happening in the other colonies. He was also one of the largest land holders in Bedford County.

John and James Piper were next to enter the fray of loud opinions. Soon they were followed by David Espy, Benjamin Elliott, Samuel Davidson, and Thomas Smith. All of these were men of account and influence in this fast-growing community.

The first generation of Pennsylvania-born-Americans was molded differently than every generation before them. The thing which had changed them the most was the recent war. Europeans expected war to be a grand pageant, fought far from home, with lofty heroes returning in glory. Artists would paint grand murals when it was done.

War on the frontier was a vicious dance with terror. Death could visit at any time of day or night. And the victims were most often women, children, and old men. It made a profound difference in the way young people perceived safety. A strong government 6,000 miles away did not make these families feel safe!

In Pennsylvania, people recognized the dependence of neighbors on each other. A new moral mindset emerged: *Social Responsibility.*

The men of Charles Cessna's generation began to value civic mindedness more than personal ambition. The core of American patriotism was born in this atmosphere of looking for leaders who place the community ahead of themselves.

Put in simple terms, while their parents had pledged to defend the King; Americans felt each man was duty bound to defend his neighbor.

John Cessna Jr. spoke at length about the corruption in English government. He had met more than a few Englishmen who had bought positions of power in the colonies. They stole everything they could to get rich, and then went back to England.

Like most colonials, John feared that the pervasive system of patronage and corruption in their homeland would ruin their new world. In England, government employees were allowed to rob and bully their constituents. They could have you jailed just for disagreeing with them, or because they wanted your possessions.

On the frontier, people wanted to be led by men who put the interests of their neighbors ahead of their own. *Public servant* was a term used to describe the ideal leader.

When Thomas Paine published his pamphlet on Common Sense, its rightness was immediately embraced by men of the frontier. Charles and John Cessna had joined frequently with their neighbors to discuss such things.

On Saturdays, farmers would meet in front of the abandoned fort and hold markets. While the wives were busy exchanging produce, crafts and goods, the men would gather in groups to discuss politics. The strongest cluster of similar minds in Bedford was the group who had migrated from Shippensburg -- the boys from Perry's Stables. They were the largest group of friends who had moved into these valleys and coves.

Many others came. But not in groups large enough to compete with the informal alliance of the men who had grown up in Shippensburg.

They were a generation with a unique outlook on life. The boys from Perry's Stables began to dominate what power there was. They elected each other to the first offices in the county. They shared like values and visions, and it was a natural thing to promote those men whom you trusted.

This meeting at the Blue Bonnet Tavern was to be the first political rally of the American Revolution as it happened in Bedford County. It had begun as an informal meeting. But William Thompson's report on what was happening in Philadelphia would polarize this community. The same was happening in villages all over the thirteen American Colonies.

Chief among the interests of John and Charles Cessna was security from the Indians. They never stopped looking to the west for the next wave of destruction. They were deeply concerned about every government interaction with the Indians that might stir up another war.

English businessmen continued to trade guns, powder, tomahawks, and scalping knives to the Indians for furs. This infuriated the men of Bedford. It was not hard to imagine that those weapons might one day be used against the farmers of Bedford County.

The people of these valleys and coves were quickly choosing sides in an argument that promised to grow ever more bitter. Frontier men wanted more say in what government did in their lives. The older and wealthier men of the community did not want to upset the powers in London, because there lay the source of all money and power.

When war started, it started in the East.

In early 1775, English Parliament had had enough of the dissidence in Boston and sent General Howe's army to place it under martial law, suspending all colonial authority. In April, he sent soldiers to Lexington and Concord to seize the militia supplies stored there, and de-fang the dissidents. Fighting erupted.

The English army was harassed all the way back to Boston, suffering heavy losses. Farmers grabbed their rifles and surrounded the city of Boston. Several thousand farmer-soldiers had penned the English Army up on Boston peninsula. Colonial leaders feared that complete anarchy would follow.

Meeting in Philadelphia for their second time, the Continental Congress voted to adopt all of the militia groups in Boston as their official army. George Washington was chosen to be the commander-in-chief. He was tasked with going there and organizing the angry farmers and hopefully preventing chaos.

Washington's first act was to ask Congress for a special weapon; an elite corps of fighting men. General Washington had spent enough time in the west to appreciate a new weapon that had been invented in Lancaster, Pennsylvania: the Rifled Gun.

It had a range three to four times greater than the military musket. And the frontiersmen of the western counties could do wondrous things with it. The new commander asked Congress to give him a battalion of six companies of sharp-shooting snipers.

In June of 1775, word reached Bedford that Congress and Washington needed volunteers for this elite group. The response was explosive.

Instead of the six companies asked for, nine companies of volunteers were raised. At Getty's Tavern (on the site of a future Gettysburg), an entire company was raised from just among the men present in the tavern. The company was filled within an hour after the news was read to them. The response in Bedford was no less enthusiastic.

In Bedford, a company was raised before sundown. Robert Cluggage was chosen as its captain. The entire community contributed to the equipment they would need, and within ten days, Cluggage and 50 men were marching towards Boston.

At first, the Public Safety Committee thought it would be a short matter for the Colonial army to convince England that negotiation was better than military occupation.

But the siege in Boston became a stalemate.

The Rifle Battalion had only been given three-month enlistments. Now those were extended to six months. And in January of 1776, they would be extended to one year.

Congress slowly realized that more militia and arms were going to be needed. Ben Franklin displayed his genius for organization with his model for a militia. It was complex, but also simple. It was also the first military draft of the new country.

The constable of each township in Pennsylvania would make a list of all able-bodied men in their jurisdiction. Field officers would be chosen by the state Committee. These officers were responsible to call a muster and organize all men into a militia structure. Each township formed a company. They could then elect their own captains and lieutenants. These captains chose the sergeants.

But the brilliance of Franklin's plan came in the next phase of organization. The men of each company were divided into eight "classes."

It was perhaps the fairest military draft that America would ever have. When his class was called, it was for two months of duty. A man could be excused if he hired a substitute, or paid a fine equal to two months pay for a substitute. Not knowing how long the war might last, it allowed each man to choose whether to serve or not.

Many adventurous young men saw an opportunity for cash by hiring out as replacements. With cash they could speed up their wait to have their own farm, wife, and family.

These battalions would meet twice a year to train and organize. The companies were made up of close neighbors and provided accountability for each other. But they would not fight together in these companies.

Franklin's plan was that community pressure would ensure that all men participated. But by calling them in classes (1 out of every 8 of their neighbors) it also assured that not too many men from one family, or a single township would be called to serve at any two-month period.

Farm production and protection of the home would not be disrupted.

Next came the selection of officers.

George Woods, John Piper, and Bernard Dougherty were recommended and chosen to serve as Colonels of the three battalions formed in

Bedford County. John Cessna was commissioned as Major and made the Adjutant of 1st Battalion. Each of these men had served terms as representatives to Pennsylvania Assembly and had good reputations. Charles Cessna, was given the rank of Major and assigned as Adjutant of 2nd Battalion.

And in the summer of 1776, shortly after the Continental Congress signed the Declaration of Independence, the first muster was held in front of Fort Bedford. Not knowing what exactly to do, this muster consisted of marking off names on the roll. Then they practiced shooting, and marching in formation (or attempting to) in a circle around the dilapidated fort.

Charles Cessna was deeply discouraged to see their appalling lack of readiness for what was coming. The officers were overwhelmed with their new responsibility. Their countrymen had declared independence and open war with the mightiest nation on earth.

Now they were watching a mob of men who had just wandered out of the woods. It was their job to transform them into an army. Charles Cessna was most disturbed by the lack of equipment. All of their weapons were one of a kind, with very questionable accuracy and in various states of repair.

While some men carried the new long rifles, many others had worn-out muskets. And a good many other men had no firearms at all, either by conscience or by poverty.

When Charles Cessna Jr. had reached the age of 10, he became his father's constant companion. The boy had amazing manners. He could sit silently for hours, never fidgeting, never crying. He merely studied his father in the throes of political discourse. Then with equal silence, he listened as his father digested the day's events on their ride home.

"Charles, it looks like we might be in a lot of trouble," the new Major said to the boy as they shared a saddle. "I don't think any one of them knows how much it will take to feed their new militia."

Charles began to estimate what these men would need by way of equipment. Canteens, cartridge boxes, blankets, coats, shoes ... there was so much needed. And from his personal experience on the Forbes Campaign of 1758, he knew that massive amounts of food were going to be needed. *It looks like people will finally appreciate all of the grain we have been storing,* he thought to himself.

Dr. Franklin's Public Safety Committee began to make requests/suggestions from each of the counties to supply the new Continental Army. In addition to wagon loads of grain, Bedford County was asked to immediately furnish 100 firelock muskets with bayonets and all appropriate equipment. But even this small request proved to be an overwhelming demand for resources.

On February 9th of 1776, David Espy, the Clerk, wrote to Franklin's Safety Committee pleading for patience.

We have but one Gunsmith in the County, who has engaged to make twenty-five Firelocks, and has been employed for these three or four months past, but has not got any of them completed; yet we are in hopes he will soon have the twenty-five finished. He has been very industrious to procure assistants or journeymen, in order to undertake the whole, but cannot obtain any; and we also have endeavored to employ others in the adjacent Counties, but are informed they are already engaged. We have provided leather, and have employed a saddler to make cartridge boxes, agreeable to the pattern sent to us and will take every necessary step in our power in order to have the whole completed.

And almost immediately a second, massive problem revealed itself to the rebellious colonies. THEY HAD NO GOVERNMENT. No one knew the rules.

In the January Quarter Session of 1776, the last group of government officials had taken oaths to the King of England. Now, that legal system did not exist. The courts did not know which laws still applied, so the courts simply stopped meeting. No court was held in Pennsylvania from the Spring of 1776 until January of 1778. It was a period of lawlessness.

There was in fact no governmental authority to order any military action, or taxes, or laws, or even impose the most basic social directives. Militia officers held Courts Martial for those who did not attend muster or appear when their duty was called.

A constitutional convention was called for Pennsylvania even before the ink was dry on the Declaration of Independence. John Cessna Jr. was chosen to represent the county at the State Congress.

Once again, Dr. Benjamin Franklin was chosen to be president of such an important session. In a few weeks, the delegates were able to put together a document which would be the framework for state government.

In many respects it reflected the sentiments of the frontier people, and the indication is that John Cessna was able to make the desires of his neighbors well known. John was one of those men who signed the first constitution of the state.

The new constitution granted the right to vote to every man who paid taxes, not just the landed gentry, as English law had allowed. More people would have a say in who ruled them. And their new government would be a Republic.

"The new state constitution has a Bill of Rights for every man," explained John Cessna to a crowd gathered at the Blue Bonnet. It was crowded to overflowing as everyone wanted to hear the important news. They were getting an entirely new government. He had brought several copies with him and they were being read in taverns around the county.

"The most important one is that the right to govern comes from the people not from the King," John declared.

"Well, damn! It's about time!" exclaimed Tom Coulter in one of the few moments he was in public agreement with anyone named Cessna.

"Indeed," said George Woods. "Maybe now the world will spin right side up for a change."

The sun was well up before the meeting ended and people began to make their way to their homes. The conversations around their hearths would be just as lively.

"Do you think we can make it work?" Charles asked his older brother. "It seems mighty lofty for a bunch of people that don't really have an army."

"It is definitely an issue in doubt, Charles. But can you think of any other kind of government that would be worth what we are risking? We are on a course of no return at this point. I heard more than one man say, we will hang together or we will hang separately."

Charles could tell that his brother was deeply troubled by the things he had seen and heard in Philadelphia. Having been to the capital himself, it was easy to imagine the debate and arguments that his brother had witnessed.

Everyone who came back from that place was as shaken as if they had ridden inside one of the tornadoes that plagued this new land. John Cessna looked exhausted, physically, and emotionally.

"Well, I for one will stand firmly with you, brother," Charles offered. "You have done a good thing, as far as I am concerned. And I will give my very life to support the direction you men have taken."

John breathed easier at this encouragement.

"You have done a brave thing, brother. Father will be proud! And you know that Grand-père would be."

"I am praying so," muttered John, mostly to himself. "It may cost a lot of us our lives before it is through."

CHAPTER SEVENTEEN
The Fight for Independence

There was fight in every direction you might look!

At home, neighbor fought with neighbor about what needed to be done ... and who should pay for it. Unlike the last war, this one would be paid for directly by the people.

Previously, the King would pay for the war, then get reimbursed through future taxes. Now, it was pay as you go. Farmers who had been desperately trying to just make a livelihood, now had to stretch and sacrifice in unprecedented ways.

The people were divided between reconciliation with the King, those who wanted no part of the argument, and those who were pushing to be a new nation. And among the latter group, there were many factions pushing their passionate opinions about what the new nation should look like.

General George Washington was more than a bit overwhelmed with trying to create a real army out of the undisciplined militia men. To complicate matters, all of his volunteers were on short enlistments. This war was taking much longer than anticipated.

As the tediousness of army life, and the lack of regular pay began to wear on their spirits, more and more soldiers wanted to leave. Much of the army was starving.

Charles Cessna's worst fears came true. England opened a second front on the western settlements. Bedford was right in the middle of the killing fields.

Henry Hamilton, Lieutenant Governor of Canada, and commander at Fort Detroit, decided to pressure the Americans for a swift capitulation. "Hamilton, The Hair Buyer," as he was to become known, enlisted Indian tribes throughout Ohio and Canada to declare war on the Americans.

A new wave of Indian war parties began to pour through the mountain passes. Settlers were helpless before the invaders. Hamilton's strategy was to divert military personnel and supplies away from General Washington. It would prove just how weak the colonies really were.

In a heartless move, Henry Hamilton offered reward for any American scalp brought to him by the savages. He offered nothing for live prisoners. The warriors learned they could make more money collecting scalps than by hunting and trapping furs. So the Indians came, just as they had come twenty years earlier. This time they came only to kill.

Charles and John Cessna were able to convince the Public Safety Committee that Bedford had its own war to fight. Philadelphia stopped asking them to send men and materials to the East in support of General Washington.

It was painfully obvious that not much support would be coming from the East to help them. Washington sent Edward Hand to command the western army. It was a small force which had more than it could do just holding on to Fort Pitt.

Vast numbers of Indians surrounded the small military force. The army was hiding inside the walls of a stronghold that really wasn't very strong at all.

When they didn't succeed at breaking through the walls of Fort Pitt on the first try, the warriors simply made a new plan. They by-passed that fort and slipped into the valleys of the western townships. They came to visit terror and death on isolated families.

All of the three battalions of Bedford County's militia were employed as ranging companies. A company was supposed to have 50 men. But the population had been so diminished that they were lucky to have companies of 20 to 30 men in the field at any one time.

This meant instead of 150 men, there were only 80 to 100 men scattered across the countryside, trying to intercept 500-1000 Indians. They pursued, and when possible intercepted, raiding parties. But it was obvious that merely reacting to Indian attacks was not sufficient. A more proactive strategy was needed.

Charles Cessna stepped forward with his plan to meet the Indians at the passes and narrow places of their trails. This time he found a strong ally in Bernard Dougherty. With limited manpower, Dougherty agreed this might be the most efficient way to utilize the few fighting men that were available.

Together they persuaded Colonels Woods and Piper to place companies of men in the various passes. The success was remarkable. But it was also short lived.

The Indians had been coming in small raiding parties of 20 or less. After a few discouraging skirmishes with the militia, the warriors began to combine parties and come in groups of no less than 100. The advantage turned against the Americans.

Supplying the troops in remote locations proved to be as difficult as Cessna had been cautioned. Colonel Dougherty and Major Cessna drafted this appeal to Philadelphia:

B. Dougherty and C. Cessna to V.P. Potter, 1781, Sir, Concerning the agreement made by us and entered into the council books, a doubt has been suggested on account of carriage. The only place in our county fit for storing provisions in, is the town of Bedford, which is in every direction, a considerable distance from such places as are capable of making the necessary defense. It is 55 miles distant from Lead Mine Gap, 40 miles from the gap of Frankston, and also 40 miles from Conemaugh. These are the common passes through which the enemy penetrates into the country. And sending provisions to all or any
of these posts will be attended with expenses, which might be entirely out of our power to defray. To neglect giving this information to the council would be in some measure criminal in us; for as much as the want of such knowledge might lead to great mistakes, by which expectations would take place, and of course disappointments ensue very interesting to the distressed Frontiers; for unless punctuality is observed, it will frustrate and render useless the salutary measures adopted by Government for the Defense of the Frontiers; we therefore pray

the sense of his Excellency and the Honorable Board of Council on this subject. We are, your obedient, humble servants,
Bernard Dougherty, and Charles Cessna

Col. Charles Cessna was appointed as purchaser for Bedford county. He had to orchestrate buying all of the food and equipment needed to keep ranging companies in the field. Charles Cessna worked tirelessly to gather and send supplies needed to protect his community. But his organizational skill was frequently tested to the breaking point.

Elizabeth became his source of emotional strength. "It is a good thing you are doing, Mr. Cessna," she would tell him.

Usually she was brushing away the curling lock of hair from the middle of his forehead. She always punctuated that action with a gentle kiss to the knife scar that was there. "If you weren't there, nothing would get done. Fret not the nay say-ers, my husband. You know what needs doing."

And the visage of Charles Cessna Jr. haunted him. He was fighting for the future of his children. Charles Jr. never argued with his father. But he never stopped watching him either. Those eyes were silently demanding in their admiration of the patriarch. Living up to his son's expectations was becoming more of a driving force in Charles' life.

In October of 1777, Charles Cessna was elected to represent Bedford county in the new State House. His term of service began the following January. Several factors pushed him into this office. The first was his frequently loud argumentation with his neighbors about what was needed in order to protect this county from Indian attack.

The second was quite simply that everyone had much more on their schedule than they could handle. Few men wanted the job. Since Charles Cessna had a lot of big ideas, let him go argue with the politicians in Philadelphia.

Those who had once served as representatives were frantically trying to organize their personal interests, while carrying out the public duties they had accepted. No one really wanted to be away from their farms and businesses when so much trouble was happening. Being a State Representative was a frustrating and thankless job.

For Charles Cessna, it meant moving back and forth between his home and Philadelphia every few weeks. He had been chosen to leave his family, and go down to play politician in the capital. It was a 200 mile trip, regardless of the weather.

On his first trip, he took Charles Jr. to serve as a personal aide, and give the boy an education that would be unrivaled among his peers.

That is when Col. Charles Cessna met Benjamin Franklin in all of his glory. Benjamin Franklin and his son, William, were among the government servants constantly moving between the state and colonial assemblies. They sought both to gather knowledge and plant wisdom in the minds of those who were leading both assemblies. Public Safety was one of their favorite topics.

Franklin stumbled upon Charles Cessna on his second day in the capital. Cessna found himself immediately under Franklin's spell. It was as though the man from Bedford had fallen into a social trap which had been waiting for him.

"The new Representative from Bedford, you say? Well, we have been waiting to meet you!" Franklin pronounced this in a loud voice as though he were announcing a long-awaited guest at a banquet. You have to come with me, young sir, I have so many questions for you to answer. You must dine with me tonight."

Grabbing his arm, Mr. Franklin pulled him through the crowd and headed for a nearby tavern. But it was not to dine.

They would spend several hours drinking and talking. Franklin repeatedly promised that Cessna was going to be probed for some important knowledge he possessed. But mostly the old statesman merely talked about himself and instructed the young man about his surroundings.

Franklin noticed the slight young man that was shadowing his new protégé. The boy did not speak. Servants were treated as though they were invisible for most social functions. The old statesman guessed that Charles Jr. must be a servant.

Franklin's energy and character were overpowering. His knowledge was immense and Charles developed a hunger to learn from this man. His personality was irresistible. He had a way of making you feel as though you were the most important person in his world...until you disagreed with him.

Franklin loved to meet new people. He immediately became their *best* friend. He showered them with compliments and offers of support and help.

In return, he expected that he had made another ally for when it next came time to vote on one of his pet projects.

Ben Franklin knew many ways to manipulate and influence people. It gave him power over newcomers to become their sponsor in political circles, introducing them to the important people.

It gave him prestige among his colleagues to know so many people, so intimately. He especially loved newcomers from the far western settlements. By befriending young Cessna, he was advancing the power of Ben Franklin the politician.

Charles did not miss what was happening for both his benefit and that of Mr. Franklin. He marveled at this new level of social skill he had never seen before.

"I met this fascinating young man for the first time today," said Franklin to a group of well-dressed men.

"Not really," interrupted Charles. Immediately he regretted correcting the statesman. But his elder did not miss a beat.

"Indeed, how has my memory failed me this time? Please tell us when we crossed paths before."

"It was in Shippensburg, when you and William came to talk about building stockades back in '55." Charles explained in a quiet voice. "I was standing behind my father."

Rubbing his chin, Franklin appeared to be searching deep into the recesses of his mind. Then he demonstrated the depth of his genius. "The tow-haired, blue-eyed boy who stood by the fireplace, of course! I remember thinking that it must be a pretty wise lad who understood the importance of that meeting. All the other children were out playing, but you wanted to hear everything. Now I recognized the same spirit in that lad that keeps hiding in your shadow."

Thirteen-year-old Charles Jr. began to blush at no longer being invisible.

Turning to the crowd, Franklin announced to the entire room, "I have known this remarkable young lad all his life! He is a bright star of the wilderness. Everyone should toast this Adonis who has come among us."

Before he was able to escape the company of this great man, Charles Cessna would visit no less than five different taverns and meet more individuals than he had ability to remember. About 10 o'clock, Franklin finally ordered the dinner he had promised.

Charles did recognize some of the names of prominent politicians and soldiers from all over the Americas. Philadelphia was filled with not only delegates to Pennsylvania's congress, but men from all over the colonies. They had come for the Continental Congress. You could not push your way through a crowd without bumping into somebody of great reputation.

At some point, Ben asked him about the scar in the corner of his forehead. He loved the story behind it. It immediately became a game he and the young man would play to impress their audience. "Mr. Cessna, where did you get that marvelous scar on your brow?"

"I was with General Forbes when he marched to Fort Duquesne in '58. An Indian took a notion to lift my hair. But I managed to keep it."

"You dare say!" exclaimed Franklin in false shock every time Charles recounted the story. "My word, you couldn't have been more than a mere boy."

"I was seventeen."

And Mr. Franklin would then raise a hero's cheer among the crowd. He praised Mr. Cessna's prowess as an Indian fighter. The truth did not matter to him so much as the impression made by his theatrics.

Charles ended the night feeling as though he had been an actor on a stage the entire evening. He was the supporting character for Ben Franklin's leading role. This was only the first of several days of such theatrics.

Franklin ushered Charles to a tailor, and carefully chose a political costume which would define Cessna's character. A gentlemen's hunting outfit created the perfect blend of educated gentlemen and woodland philosopher. A fur cap completed the look.

Charles made a wonderful first impression in capitol society, because of Mr. Franklin's tutelage. In one meeting when they were discussing the Red Man, Charles bragged to the group how Ben and William Franklin had saved hundreds of lives with their efforts to get the frontier settlements to build stockades.

Franklin loved to hear compliments like this, especially when made in public places. Cessna was invited to sit and drink with the group discussing defense and security issues.

"This new colonial script isn't going to get us far," John Dickenson told a table full of delegates from three states. "We have no gold or silver to back it up. No one wants to accept it."

"Aye," said a man that Cessna did not recognize. "None of the farmers in New York want to sell any food or fodder to our army. We have caught them sneaking it to the British Army because the Red Coats pay with coin. The same is true in Pennsylvania. These damned Quakers don't care which side eats as long as they get rich themselves."

The group began to grouse loudly in protest. Dickenson, a Quaker, was red-faced.

Charles Cessna had seen the same thing in Bedford County. The government had a lengthy list of needs, but only had paper money to pay for it. Charles had to admit he was reticent about accepting it himself.

"Well, we have got to make them!" Franklin roared. "It is the only way we can win this war. Besides, if everyone in the colonies holds state notes, they won't want to see us lose.

"These are small loans if you will. And when a man is owed enough money by a government, he naturally doesn't want to see that government fail. He would lose his money. *Where your treasure is, there your heart is.*"

Franklin lectured for another hour about how important it was for government officials to hold fast in making people take Pennsylvania script instead of coin. He indicated that bullying farmers into selling grain for script was in everyone's their best interest. Cessna left that evening not sure of which direction was right.

CHAPTER EIGHTEEN
Congress

The convening day of Pennsylvania's congress was unlike anything Charles Cessna had experienced before. The pageantry was extravagant and lavish, despite the hardship of war.

The Supreme Executive Council sent out a notice to all participants that the parade to the swearing-in ceremony would look like this:

Agreed, that the order of the procession to the courthouse be as follows, viz:
Constables with their staves,
Sub-Sheriffs with their wands,
High Sheriff with his wand,
Coroner with his wand,
Judges of the Supreme Court,
Prothonotary of the Supreme Court,
Judge, Register, and Marshal of the
*   Admiralty, Naval Officer,*
Treasurer and Attorney General of the
*   State,*
Secretary of the Land office, Receiver &
Surveyor General of the State,
Justices of the Peace,
Prothonotary of the Court of Common,
Clerk of Court of Quarter Sessions,
Clerk of the City court,
Master of the Rolls & Escheator General,

Secretary of the Council,
His Excellency the President, and
      Honorable the vice President
Members of the Council, two by two,
Sergeant-at-Arms with the Mace,
The Honorable Speaker of the House of
    Assembly,
Clerk of the House,
Members of the House of Assembly,
    two by two, (including Charles Cessna)
Doorkeeper of the general Assembly,
Provost and Faculty of the University,
General and field officers of the militia,
Such citizens as desire.

It was quite a spectacle indeed!

Charles Cessna Jr. was perched in a tree as the parade made its way down the boulevard. He supposed that it was grander than any coronation in London. And he swelled with immense pride when his father marched by.

For the first time in his life, Charles Cessna was given a hero's welcome. Franklin's final gift to his young colleague was to insist that he buy another suit of clothes before he returned to the wilderness. Nothing less would do than the suit appropriate for a lawyer.

"Wear it whenever you do your work as a commissioner. The costume is important for the occasion. Trust me," Franklin cajoled.

A much more sophisticated, skilled, and wise Charles Cessna would return to his hometown. Some of his neighbors thought his new suit was just "putting on airs" after having been to the capitol. But even his critics admitted that he had demonstrated the education and political acumen of the budding statesmen. He grew in public esteem.

CHAPTER NINETEEN
Bloody Days

Charles Cessna's life became a confusing time between two very different worlds.

When he was in Philadelphia, he was expected to be one of the well dressed, and well spoken members of the gentry. There was ample food and drink at every tavern. There was no sign of the desperation and sacrifice being made by the common man in the countryside.

No one seemed in a hurry to get much done. In fact, it took what seemed an impossibly long time to get any decisions made. Even Ben Franklin, the president of the Pennsylvania Assembly did not seem in a rush to make some decisions.

But in between his visits to Philadelphia, Charles Cessna lived in a much different world. Bedford County was in the middle of a war. Worse, it was on the very edge of the battle lines. Every decision was urgent and every action should have been taken yesterday!

War parties were making frequent incursions, leaving bodies, and burning cabins behind them. Charles was now a Lt. Colonel and 2nd in command of the 1st Battalion of Bedford Militia. He was under continual pressure to make quick decisions about where companies should be stationed.

There was no time for considered and polite debate when you are sending men into battle. Choices have to be made quickly. Choices which meant life or death for your neighbors and friends.

As the purchaser for county and military supplies, Charles was under continual pressure to find and buy as much food as possible. He needed to find new sources for everything his men would need when they were in the field.

Charles was continually at odds with the state commissary in Philadelphia. On his frequent visits he spent more time arguing over shipments of shoes, guns, powder, shot, and clothing than he did in actually attending the political debates on the State House floor.

There was no time for Charles Cessna to rest. Each time he was able to visit his home Elizabeth scolded him that he was trying to do too much. Charles had to agree with her. But there was so much to be done. And Bedford county was short on leadership and manpower.

About a third of the men in Bedford had sided with those loyal to the King. In the early days of the war, they had resisted every effort that Charles Cessna was making. Finally, these Tories just quit the county altogether, taking with them many of the things Charles would need to do his job.

A considerable number of the younger men had been taken by Washington to serve in the Continental Army. Those left behind to defend the frontier were few in number, and poor in equipment.

It was a challenge for Col. Cessna. Each month, he had to travel to Philadelphia for a few weeks of making laws. Then he had to rush back to make sure that each new change of militia was ready to march.

Every two months, Charles Cessna was responsible for organizing the new companies coming on to duty. He had to equip and supply them with the food and clothing they would need. Then he had to assign them to some remote pass where they might intercept war parties. There were far more places needing guards than he had men to send there.

Charles was so short of supplies that on many occasions, he had to take the rifles and shoes from men coming off of their two month duty, and give them to men just coming on duty.

Col. Charles Cessna lived under continual pressure. He was trying to help the state create a new system of government. At the same time, he was in constant search for the food and materials needed by his soldiers. These were things which were needed for the survival of his family and their friends.

Every eight weeks there was a frenzied effort to prepare the new companies for service, and to pay the men just being relieved of duty. And in between each of those jobs he faced angry complaints and criticism from those he was trying to serve.

Had Elizabeth not been the loving and patient supporter Charles needed, he might have come unraveled completely. Somehow she knew when he was at his breaking point. Somehow she filled the empty place he left in the family's affairs. Somehow she kept Charles Jr. and their one slave focused on keeping the farm running.

As soon as the snow disappeared, the Indians began their springtime raids. Death seemed to be lurking at every cabin door. The Indians adjusted to Charles' efforts of placing companies of rangers at the passes.

Now they came in groups of 100 or more. Frequently the ranging companies were outnumbered. And the inevitable massacre finally happened to one of Charles' companies.

On Saturday, July 15, 1780, Col. Cessna suffered the greatest loss of his command. He had ordered a company to go to the relief of a terrified group of settlers at Shoup's Fort. Captain Phillips and 19 men rushed to the aid of their neighbors, but did not make it. As they circled around Tussey Mountain near its southern end, they came to the Heater family farm.

It was snowing heavily and the company sought shelter in the abandoned house. The sunrise held no comfort for them. The first to leave the cabin on Sunday morning discovered that they were surrounded by a force of at least 80 warriors.

One of the survivors would later tell that two men of their attackers were not Indians. These were their Tory neighbors from Bedford, who had abandoned them. Now they were coming back, bringing the savages to get revenge on their former friends.

A four-hour fight broke out that ended with the Americans' surrender as the cabin was burned down around them. Two Indians had been killed and two wounded at that point, but none of the Rangers was harmed.

Taken prisoner, the Rangers were divided into two groups. Captain Phillips, his son, and eight others were taken to Detroit and given to the British as prisoners of war. They returned after the fighting ended in 1782. But they were starved and in sickly condition.

The other group of ten was not so lucky. All were led into the woods with their hands tied behind them. They had traveled barely a mile before their captors decided they were too slow. The ten rangers were tied to trees and at least four volleys of arrows were loosed into their bodies. They were scalped and left hanging from the trees as a warning.

Lieutenant Colonel Charles Cessna headed the column that came searching for Phillips' company. His heart sank at the discovery of the mutilated bodies. Charles knew each of these men personally. He had ordered them on this mission. He would have to report to their wives and parents.

As he was surveying the scene of the massacre, another company of rangers emerged from the forest. Captain Samuel Mason and his men had been in the field for two weeks chasing the same war party which had done this terrible thing. Mason's company were men from the townships just south of Fort Pitt.

Captain Mason arrived just in time to rescue Col. Cessna from his despondence. Charles' confidence had been shaken badly by the bloody scene before him. The appearance of this bold and confident young warrior was an encouragement to him.

Mason and Cessna chose to bury the bodies where they fell, because the woods were yet full of danger. Charles was in a hurry to get his men back to the safety of a fort. Mason's company accompanied them back to Bedford where Col. Cessna could replenish their supplies.

Charles returned to Bedford feeling the loss of his men, and knowing he had failed in his leadership of them. It took two full days to visit every home that had lost a soldier. His despair was deep. It took Elizabeth many weeks to console him.

CHAPTER TWENTY
"I've Lost It All!"

In April of 1780, Charles Cessna was again appointed the Commissioner of Purchasing for the County. Charles received orders to purchase *25 tons of hay (at £6 per ton), 2 thousand bushels of corn (at 4 shillings per), and 4 thousand bushels of oats (at 2 shillings 6 pence per.)*

And he was given a small fortune in Pennsylvania script to purchase it with, it was a daunting task.

In addition to government work, he still had to manage and continue developing his farm. He was also Lt. Colonel of the 1st Battalion of Bedford Militia. But he could no longer serve as the Representative to the State Assembly. He did not have the time or energy.

Because farmers were not coming forward voluntarily to sell their crops, Col. Cessna needed men he could trust to serve as enforcers. With their support, he traveled to the remote farms to find what was required.

Bernard Dougherty was his first choice as an agent to purchase from area farmers. His second choice was his own son. At the age of just 18, Charles Cessna Jr. received a brevet appointment as Captain in the Militia. Normally this rank was given by election of the men in a company. But Charles Jr. was not responsible for leading men in battle. His rank merely gave him military authority over those of his neighbors whom he was buying food from. They were all members of the militia. His rank enabled him to pressure, bully or coerce the cooperation he needed. He outranked every farmer he would meet.

The local farmers were not eager to provide supplies to the government. In fact, most were downright resentful and resistant to the idea. Many hid their surplus grain and livestock so the county officers could not force them into surrendering it.

The government dictated the prices they would pay, not allowing any negotiation or free market pricing. And the government insisted on paying in paper money which quickly lost its value and was difficult to pass on.

In the only time his words are recorded for history, Captain Charles Cessna Jr. wrote a desperate letter to Col. James Morgan, the superintendent of purchasers for Pennsylvania. He outlined the frustrations of the job his father had given him.

The Bearer, Mr. Isaac Worrell one of my deputies in the purchasing way in this county goes to you with the express purpose of getting your advice in order to direct and govern me in the Departments. The distress of this County is truly great, Murders and depredations are committed almost every week, and not a single Article can be had for the Money that's now current: I am even threatened and inveighed against by the people, for not having suitable provisions for such as do Military duty, and it is impossible for me to get it for the Money I have; I am indebted to numbers in Consequence of such articles as we purchased and so are my Deputies, having engaged on the Credit of the Money with which is now useless; and unless something be done in order to enable us to get provisions for such as are employed in protecting the County, I am afraid the settlement brake up totally and that very soon. It is impossible for me to send you an accurate Return having purchased on the credit of the Money which was in so fluctuating a state while it dubiously passed as to leave no room for a certain price in any Article; and now no person wou'd (sic) receive any quantity of it for a single Beef Cattle, I beg you wil (sic) dispatch the Bearer with all due haste and I hope in such a manner equipped as will enable me and those that are employed by me in the service to do the requisite and necessary Duty expected of us. I am sire, with great respect, Your most obed't H'ble serv't. ...Chas Cessna, Capt."

Lt. Colonel Charles Cessna made many enemies and few friends as he coerced much needed food from his reluctant neighbors. When a farmer realized that he had traded his crop for now worthless paper money, he focused his resentment on the individual who had given him that money.

Many of them felt they had been robbed by a man they had previously considered a friend, and even respected. A politician was not going to win many votes by forcing farmers to sell at fixed prices, for a currency that no one wanted.

"Colonel Cessna, there has been trouble!"

Matthew Dougherty had arrived at the Bedford County Building in a great hurry. It was obvious he was bringing unwelcome news.

"Captain Cessna has been hurt." Dougherty continued. "The storm last night caused a flash flood on the Juniata. Young Charles was coming back from the Snake Spring (township) and got caught in it. His horse washed out from under him and he near drowned."

Charles Cessna found it difficult to breathe and impossible to talk as he received the report from young Dougherty. He had never considered that this job might cost his son's life.

Charles could do nothing but wait until his son was carried back to town in a borrowed wagon. The only doctor in town was waiting for that wagon to arrive. The men who had been helping Captain Charles Cessna began to tell the story.

"We were buying oats from the farmers around Snake Spring. They were an uncooperative bunch. I thought the weather looked bad and we had better head home early."

"Charles made one more call because he said he didn't want to have to come all the way back again," John added. "Mr. Fredigut was particularly stubborn and hard to deal with, so it took us longer than usual. '

"By the time we reached the Juniata," continued Samuel, "the water was higher than the horses could wade. When Charles' horse started to swim, it floundered and dumped him in the current. Colonel, the current was so fast that it took us almost half an hour to catch up to him and pull him out. He had so much river in him...."

The man could not continue because of the tears in his voice. The doctor was able to bring young Cessna around. Charles' heart calmed when he heard his son speak for the first time. It was like having him come back from the dead.

But his first words would hit his father like an axe handle. "I lost it all!" Captain Cessna told his father. "I lost the saddle bag with the money and the receipts. I tried to swim after it, but it got away from me."

This bag represented a small fortune. Its loss would be enough to ruin their family. Without the receipts and the remaining currency, Charles would be responsible for repaying the government over £1,200.

Considering how much the family had already lost by accepting worthless money themselves, and other sacrifices they had made, this could mean bankruptcy. Charles Jr. had risked his life to try to save his family from disaster. He understood that loosing this one bag, was tantamount to "losing it all."

It took several days for the boy to recover. During that time, his father and others were scouring the woods beside the Juniata River, searching frantically for the lost saddle bag.

They returned to Elizabeth's cabin in a state of hopelessness. Even young Charles' recovery could not cheer their defeated spirits.

What none in the community knew, was that William Fredigut had found the saddlebag the next morning. He was still bristling mad that he had been forced to sell his cash crop of oats at such a low price. And to boot, he had to sell it for something he knew was worthless.

Fredigut felt, and not unreasonably so, that he had been robbed of a year's labor. Looking through the contents of the saddleback he realized the opportunity before him.

He could un-write the previous day's transaction. When they came to pick up his oats, he could deny ever having sold it, or having received payment. Carefully he burned the receipt he had given Captain Cessna and the remaining cash from the saddlebag. He also burned the receipts his neighbors had given Cessna. A thousand pounds of Continental Script went up in smoke.

When the deed was done, Fredigut began to feel some remorse. He eventually confessed the thing to his cousin, Tom Coulter. Coulter realized the advantage it gave him over his old adversary, Charles Cessna. He advised Fredigut to keep quiet about it.

It was a secret that gave each of them certain power. And such power might be useful in the future. In the meantime they could watch Col. Cessna struggle.

In the office his wife had built for him, Col. Charles Cessna agonized over his accounting books. He had been given money by the government to purchase desperately needed materials.

It did not matter to the government that they had given him worthless money. Pennsylvania expected an accurate accounting of every half-pence. He must return either the cash, or receipts showing where it was spent. Now there was a huge deficit.

He had kept duplicate records in his office, so the only thing which was really lost was the receipts from the past few days, and what cash remained in the saddle bag.

But that was almost £1,200 that he was responsible for. His dilemma was great. It would cost everything he had to make up such a great amount. And he would still be short on the debt. Now began the devil's dance in the head of Charles Cessna.

It is not fair that my family should lose everything just because I was trying to serve our country. It doesn't make sense that I should have to pay for all this. There has got to be a way I can fix this problem. There has got to be a way.

Charles Jr. was in abject grief over the pain his mistake had caused his father. He had only wanted to make the old man proud of him, now he had brought certain disaster on the family.

Charles Cessna entered another period of major depression. His son's broken spirit only added to Charles' devastated mood.

There has got to be something I can do.

Charles Cessna made a bad choice.

Convincing himself that no one would ever find out, he hatched a plan to rescue himself.

Charles Jr. would recreate from memory all of the receipts he had been given in that last two days. Charles, Sr. would forge the signatures of the farmers who had received payment. To make up for most of the cash which had been lost, they would fabricate a receipt to themselves.

And Col. Charles would take all of the £231 he had in the family treasury to provide the rest.

In his mind he rationalized it as the best solution to the problem. He convinced himself that it was the "right" way to handle it. It would prove to be the worst decision of his life.

In 1782, the war ended. Charles Cessna completed his tenure as Purchasing Commissioner. He was again nominated to serve as Representative to the State Assembly.

His commander, Colonel George Woods, received the highest number of votes, and Cessna received the second highest. Their totals were only 6 votes apart.

Policy was that the top two vote recipients would be recommended to the Supreme Executive Council. The Council would choose which one would serve in the office. Almost always, the top vote recipient would be selected.

But this time, John Piper was a member of the Executive Council. Being from Bedford County he knew both of these men very well. He persuaded the members to choose Charles Cessna over George Woods.

The news did not sit well in Bedford County. Many people had accepted bad money for good crops. They felt that Charles Cessna was responsible for their loss. Now they wondered if he had bribed his way into this new position with money he had stolen from them.

Supporters of George Woods began a campaign to object to the selection. There were three months between the election and the day a new Representative would take office. They used those weeks to prepare an attack on Charles Cessna.

Tom Coulter and others began to take depositions of people with complaints against Col. Cessna. There were many people who had resented being forced to sell crops against their will.

Tom Fredigut stepped forward.

Fredigut claimed he had never received payment for his surplus oats. He insisted that the Cessnas had stolen his crop and forged his name on the receipt.

An investigation revealed that several of the receipts had been forged. And technically, as the accounting report which Charles Cessna had filed to the state was based on forged documents, it amounted to perjury.

An official petition of protest, with a carefully selected packet of depositions and evidence, was sent to the Supreme Executive Council. It demanded that Cessna be removed from office. It also asked that George Woods be installed as representative.

John Piper, member of the Council, defended Charles Cessna's trustworthiness. He explained the cause of some people's resentments of him. Piper convinced the Council to table the protest and do nothing about it.

A few days into the January session, George Woods appeared in person at the door of the Executive Council. He demanded that the Council forward the petition to the Speaker of the House for action against Cessna.

The Council informed Mr. Woods that they intended to do nothing with the petition unless the Speaker of the House asked for it.

So, George Woods, Tom Coulter, and several others went across the square to the Pennsylvania House of Assembly. Within 24 hours they had stirred up enough excitement that the Speaker sent a formal request to the Supreme Executive Council asking for the petition and depositions which accused Col. Charles Cessna of misdeeds.

In the next day's session, the Honorable Charles Cessna was censured. A vote removed him from office. Minutes of the Assembly record that a committee was formed to investigate him. The supervisor of purchases was ordered to present all of Mr. Cessna's receipts and records on the desk of the Speaker.

CHAPTER TWENTY-ONE
Shame

Charles Cessna returned to Bedford in shame. The Executive Supreme Council retaliated against Col. Woods by refusing to allow him to fill Cessna's seat in the Assembly. They chose to let that position remain vacant for the entire year. Still, Woods and Coulter felt victorious.

Unlike the swiftness with which other crimes were prosecuted, the Supreme Executive Council seems to have been dragging its feet on the issue of Charles Cessna. Perhaps it was the influence of John Piper on that Council. Perhaps it was because the President of the Council, John Dickenson, remembered the service that Cessna had provided during the war.

Whatever the reason, the recommendation of the Assembly to prosecute Cessna was again tabled in the Supreme Council. No action was taken until September 11, 1783. Then the investigating committee visited the Supreme Council as a group, and laid out the details of the charges.

After that, the Supreme Council was forced to act. The Attorney General was ordered to pursue charges of forgery and perjury against Colonel Charles Cessna.

Charles Cissna, the former member of the Assembly, and former Commissioner of Purchases for Bedford County, was branded a criminal.

John Piper sent a personal letter to Charles, advising him of what had happened, and what would happen next. Charles Sr. and Jr. sat in the gloom of the office reviewing all that this letter meant.

"I am so sorry, Paw! This is all my fault. I should have tied the bag onto the saddle. It would never have come loose if I had been more careful."

"It isn't your fault, Charles." The heart of a father was breaking. "Such things happen in war."

His mind sifted through the heavy burdens before him. His family was facing certain financial ruin. His reputation as an honorable man and public servant were forever tarnished.

If he did not handle this well, the life and reputation of his son would also be destroyed. There seemed to be no way out of the mess he was in.

"Can't we just borrow the money and pay it back?" young Charles asked. "It's not but a few hundred pounds. Surely we can raise that. You have a lot of friends, paw."

"None of our friends and family have any money to spare, son. This war has left all of us on the edge of poverty. I couldn't ask any of our friends to help. And besides, it is far more than a few hundred pounds."

"What do you mean?"

"The charges of forgery and perjury are felonious. It will cost a lot of money to defend against them. If I am found guilty, it means a certain prison sentence. How will I care for your mother and the girls if I am in prison?

"And it is not just us who are in danger, son. Your uncle John and Mr. Dougherty signed my bond for £500. The courts will sue them for that amount, AND try to take their land. My problems may just end up destroying all three of us."

Charles Jr. sat stunned at the news his father had given him. It had seemed like such a small mistake, and made for good reasons. There had been no intention to steal.

"But that is so much more than the amount of money that went missing. How can they ask for so much?" the young man asked.

"Once they establish that I falsified records, it raises the question as to how much more is missing, stolen, or lost. The Attorney General is likely to go after every penny he can get for the government."

"What can I do, Paw? I can tell them it was my fault." Charles Jr. had a broken look about him. It was clear he was taking the entire guilt on himself.

"Son, it was my own choice to cover up the loss and to manipulate the records. It was my decision ... my responsibility ... you had nothing to do with it. I will figure it out, somehow."

And Charles conceived a plan that would settle the issue. It would leave only him the worst for it. He had to spare his brother and Bernard Dougherty from being punished for his error.

Charles Cessna agreed to offer title to his farm in Cumberland Valley as reimbursement and penalty. The court would sell it, and the government would keep all the proceeds.

But most important for his political foes, Charles would leave Bedford County and never seek public office again. In exchange, no recourse would be sought against those who posted his bond.

His brother and friend would be spared any further liability on his behalf. Only his estate would be forfeited. However, the greatest loss would be in the relationship with his son.

Their bond was broken. Charles began to avoid his son. Their conversations became short, and happened only when it was essential.

For Charles, his shame made it difficult to look his son in the eyes. Those eyes in which he had imagined so many questions in the past, now became a reflection of his failure. He just could not stand to look at them.

Charles Jr. thought his father's emotional withdrawal was because the son was being blamed for the loss. It became hard for him to be alone with his father.

Young Charles knew his father to be an honest and heroic man. Now the sins of the son had tarnished the nobility of the father. It was a weight which he would find difficult to bear.

Word of the agreement quickly reached the leadership in Philadelphia. Col. Charles Cessna had more than one friend in America's new capitol. Charles received a personal letter from General Nathanael Greene.

At the conclusion of the war, the state of Georgia sought to bolster its population. They had offered General Greene, the beloved hero of Yorktown, a large section of land for him to retire to.

The state also offered a bounty of "Head Rights Grants" to any veteran of the war who wished to relocate there. Officers of Colonel Charles Cessna's rank were given large tracts of land.

Under the Head Rights Grants, anyone who presented a letter from their commanding officer, testifying to their service, was entitled to 200 acres of free land. An extra 50 acres was promised for every member of your household, including slaves. Charles Cessna had quite a large list of dependents at this time.

Late in 1783, Pennsylvania conducted a count of "Persons and Property". In Cumberland Valley Township of Bedford County, Charles Cessna is listed as owning 300 acres, with 10 white souls and 1 slave living in his house.

Among the family that he and Elizabeth were caring for were their children: Charles Jr., John, Samuel, Robert, Elizabeth, Mary, Catherine, John's wife, and "Rube," the slave man who ran his farm.

Charles Cessna was looking for a fresh start. Greene County, Georgia offered him a chance to recoup his losses, and start with a new reputation.

Charles organized his own expedition to make the migration. Before the first frost of 1783, Charles Cessna was leading a large group down the Great Wagon Road from Gettysburg, Pennsylvania to Agusta, Georga.

The party included several neighbors.

Charles Cessna Jr. had to remain behind. He would operate the farm, protecting its worth, until it had been sold. Diligent in this regard, he continued to raise crops and pay taxes until a buyer was found. It took several years.

On 19 March 1786, the Carlisle *Gazette* ran the following advertisement.

Sale of Plantation of late property of Charles Cessna, esq, in Cumberland Valley, on the Great Road from Bedford to Cumberland.

*300 acres. Apply to Thomas Coulter, esq.
Who lives near the premises, or George
Funk in Bedford; or Thos. Smith, James
Hamilton, or Thos. Duncan in Carlisle.*

All five of these men are recorded as billing the Pennsylvania government for their efforts to sell the property.

When at last the farm had sold, and all matters were made right, Charles Jr. could not bring himself to join his father in Georgia.

Whether it was his sense of guilt, or the fact that he had started his own family, he was never reunited with his father.

Charles Cessna, Jr. married Rebecca Culbertson, a niece of his mother, and daughter of their neighbor Robert Culbertson. She was his first cousin. They established their own farm and lived out their lives in Bedford County.

CHAPTER TWENTY-TWO
"Will We Find Peace?"

"**W**ill we find peace in this new place, Mr. Cessna?" Snuggled alongside him, with her chin perched on his chest, Elizabeth smiled at her husband.

This had to be the best time of the day.

Lying on their pallet beneath the wagon, waiting to start the day, every morning seemed bright with promise.

The early morning light always made those eyes of hers seem more magical.

Those eyes! Charles thought to himself. *A man can find strength just looking into those eyes.*

"I certainly hope so, Mrs. Cessna. Everyone in Greene county will be new, starting over just like us. So, none of the problems of the past two years should follow us."

He said this both as a prayer to God, and as a promise to his wife. "And besides, the Indians down there are much more peaceful than the ones in Pennsylvania."

"Well, our children sure are excited about the new place" Elizabeth said. Have you noticed how much time Samuel has been spending around the Baker wagon?"

Col. Charles Cessna, Sr. and his family were now a part a wagon train of 40 families, headed for a new life in Georgia. Robert Baker, was from Cumberland County, and his family had joined Col. Cessna's group at Getty's Tavern.

"Do you suppose he has taken a fancy to that Polly Baker?" Charles asked. Then in a tease he added, "Or maybe he just likes Mrs. Baker's cooking better than yours."

The last comment earned him a pretend punch in the nose. And he held his bride tightly as she struggled against him.

I love this woman! he comforted himself.

The journey from Pennsylvania to Georgia was transformative for them. The road was easy. And it was like being reborn in so many ways.

There was relief as they left the criticism and social stings of a bitter seven-year war behind them. Charles felt as though he had been laboring under a heavy load that had broken him in the end.

Elizabeth Cessna watched as her husband slowly fought his way out of a deep depression. He was beginning to talk with excitement and energy again. Charles Cessna was again discussing the future with a sense of optimism in his voice. As hard as it had been to leave everything, Elizabeth was happy they had made the choice to start over.

Ever the astute businessman, Charles had a plan to recover his financial losses. Scraping together what extra cash he could, he had brought a valuable cargo with them. Four hundred pounds of lead, and four casks of black powder rode snugly in their wagon.

During the war he learned that such cargo could double and triple its value the farther from civilization you went. And by carrying this cargo to the back woods of Georgia, he would more than recover the expenses of their move.

At Getty's Tavern, where the caravan was being organized for the long trip, Col. Cessna had also managed to purchase some saw blades from a Dutch man. Brought from the Netherlands, these were the kinds of tools used to make a carpenter shop. Though he did not have the knowhow for such things, Charles reasoned that they might be a wise investment.

Samuel Cessna was indeed enamored by Polly Baker. They shared the same indomitable spirit, and an unbridled energy that kept either of them from staying in one place more than two minutes.

Both loved to explore. Neither of them liked being told they could not do something. They seemed made for each other. Although those made wise by age, wondered how the two would ever be able to get along in such an energetic relationship.

The wagon train stopped at Fincastle, Virginia to rest. Rest was needed to prepare for the climb up to Roanoke Gap on the Blue Ridge.

Polly announced that she wanted a "church wedding." She declared that the church in Fincastle was the most beautiful she had ever seen.

Her parents thought it a pretty ordinary-looking chapel, but they had long ago learned to be careful about picking their arguments with her.

Samuel and Polly crossed the Blue Ridge as husband and wife. Charles and Elizabeth held optimistic hopes for happy years ahead of them. The empty place created by leaving Charles Jr. behind, was quickly being filled by their noisy daughter-in-law.

The travel served to bind the travelers together in a way that a sense of community would exist by the time they reached their destination.

A substantial portion of Washington County, Georgia had been surveyed in 1784. It was being doled out to war veterans through the Head Rights Grant program. The plan was to name the new area, Greene County.

The influx of new settlers was anything but orderly. The only thing required to get a grant was to have a letter signed by your commanding officer testifying that you had served. Some unscrupulous officers were providing such letters for anyone who would pay their price. Some less-than-honest land officers were passing out far more grants for land than there was land to be settled.

From the beginning, the confusion was great, and the arguments over land were frequent.

But one thing was certain … only land on the east side of the Oconee River had been approved for settlement. The Creek Nation had passionate feelings about where the boundary lay.

No whites were allowed on the west side of the river.

Charles Cessna soon had his first experience with "The Civilized Tribes." In Pennsylvania, one seldom saw an Indian unless he was on a murderous rampage. In Georgia, the Cherokee and Creek Indians expected to be more assimilated into white culture, and moved freely between the two. They also engaged the white settlers in frequent argument about proper ways the land was to be used.

The free land was being overfilled quickly. Unhappy, settlers began to eye the pristine property across the river.

In 1786 a number of community leaders met with a group of Creek chiefs and made the Treaty of Shoulder Bone Creek. It opened land for settlement near Greensboro, but on the west side of the Oconee.

Immediately there was conflict. These were not government officials. Nor were the Indians the principal chiefs of the Creek nation. Neither side had any authority to make this treaty.

In a move that Charles Cessna had never conceived of, the true leaders of the Creek Nation sent a delegation to the Georgia Governor protesting the treaty. When the Governor declined to hear them, the delegation went to Philadelphia and appealed directly to the fledgling United States Congress.

Congress was not anxious to start another Indian War. They voided the treaty as not being made with an appropriate government authority.

The people of Greene County were incensed. Citizens all across the southern states were enraged that Congress thought it could interfere with local matters.

A number of white settlers just moved over the river anyway and laid claim to new lands. Samuel Cessna was one of those bold interlopers.

In early spring 1786, Samuel Cessna had finished his cabin and was away from his cabin clearing land for planting. A small group of Creek hunters happened onto his homestead. They found Polly busily making the forest look like a "civilized place."

Without any pretense of politeness, they began to deride this white woman for being where she should not be. In their own language they began to tell her she was trespassing and would have to move ... and move quickly.

One thing Polly Cessna was known for was her temper. She frequently entered fiery debate with people of authority.

Not understanding the language, Polly had no trouble understanding the threatening tone in which they addressed her. So, she returned their angry speech with an even more venomous diatribe of her own.

Had they fully understood her insults they might have taken a more aggressive action than they did. One warrior thought it sufficient to step forward and slap this disrespectful woman.

An infuriated Polly ran into her cabin and emerged in a blind fury, with a rifle. She was not in control of herself. The gun discharged harmlessly into the ground.

One of the braves stepped forward and clubbed her. She dropped like a stone. The warriors looked at each other in surprise. None of them had anticipated a violent confrontation, nor had they intended murder.

But not one of them had any remorse about their actions. They were there to evict a trespasser. They were in the right.

Believing they had killed the woman, one brave knelt down. With one hand he grabbed a fistful of her hair. With the other hand he made two swift circular motions with his knife. Then, giving a strong tug, he removed a good deal of her scalp.

No words need to be spoken between them, and the Indians moved into the cabin to see what booty they might find.

Polly Cessna awoke to the sound of the Indians ransacking her home. Her rifle was gone.

She leapt to her feet and began to scream for help.

She had yet to notice that she had been terribly wounded on the crown of her head. But when blood began flowing down her face, Polly began to panic.

The Indians exited the cabin. They were greeted with the sight of a scalped woman running in circles around the yard. She was alternating between screaming for help, and giving them loud threatening insults. The warriors were reduced to unbridled laughter.

It was too much for Polly.

She began to run for help. She ran as fast as she could through the woods to the closest neighbor she could think of. Mary Bridger would know what to do. So she ran to Mary's house at Cow Ford on the Oconee River.

The warriors were so astonished that they didn't think to give chase.

Mary ran the entire two miles to Cow Ford. She stumbled and fell several times. Losing so much blood made her weak. She arrived as a group of neighbors were gathering to help raise a new cabin. Among the group was her brother-in-law, John Cessna.

Polly emerged from the woods and crossed the creek. She was drenched in streams of blood. Her remaining hair was matted with red ooze. Crimson rivulets dripped down her dress giving her a ghoulish appearance that shocked the crowd of people.

"The Indians are on the War Path!" someone shouted, and panic gripped the entire group. Women and children began to scream. Men instantly went on the defensive and searched for the best way to react.

John Cessna grabbed his gun and stepped forward. "Jeb, your horse runs the fastest. You had better run and alert the neighbors. Anyone else with a gun, follow me if you have the courage." And John ran directly back down the path that Polly had just come up.

As the women gathered Polly into their arms and began to treat her wounds, John and three other men made their way to his brother's cabin.

The home was empty, but war cries could be heard echoing through the woods.

Creeping forward they discovered two pairs of warriors frantically poking a pile of brush with sticks. They killed all four of the Creek men, without suffering any wounds to themselves.

It was then John discovered his brother Samuel was beneath the brush, hiding for his life. His only weapon had been the rifle he had left with his wife. Had John Cessna and the others delayed another five minutes, Samuel would have been dead.

In triumph they returned to Cow Ford.

John was considered a hero by his community. When it came time to elect officers for the new county, John Cessna was chosen to as its first Sheriff.

The end result of that day, was War.

The attack on Polly Cessna was the opening chapter of seven years of intermittent war between the settlers and the tribes west of the Oconee River.

Tragically, it would be another attack on a second Cessna woman that would punctuate the end of hostilities.

CHAPTER TWENTY-THREE
Judge Cessna

Charles and Elizabeth Cessna came rushing when word of the attack reached them. They found their son and daughter in law at the home of her father, Robert Baker.

The girl had a large bandage around her head, but could not be calmed. Her dress still covered in blood; Polly was pacing around the yard. A curious crowd had gathered and Polly was giving loud rants about the savages. "We gotta go get 'em," she cried. After a few hours, she collapsed in exhaustion and was carried to a bed.

The event had been deeply disturbing to the community. Charles and Elizabeth returned home in a cloud of gloom. Elizabeth wept silently until past midnight. When he was certain his wife was asleep, Charles allowed himself to cry also.

He was doomed to a life of war and strife. *Is there no place where a man can live in peace?* He prayed. *Just live in peace.*

Charles' spirit was deeply burdened. He had made this long trip to find a safe home for his family. Now it seemed that war, especially war with the Indians was not to be escaped.

He considered moving again. But where could he go?

Back to Pennsylvania? Down to Savannah? There are going to be difficulties anywhere I go. We would be better off if I just stayed here and made this place peaceful. But it ain't going to be easy!

In the early morning hours he made his decision to be a public figure again. He would work for peace.

Whites were angered that a defenseless woman had been attacked. Creeks were deeply wounded by the "murder" of four of their finest young men.

Wise men of both sides sought to cool tempers, but to no avail.

The Indians staged a raid in retaliation. The white settlers retaliated against that raid with another of their own. Which in turned earned another Indian attack. And so it escalated.

A few weeks after the assault on Polly Cessna, Creek warriors attacked and burned the new town of Greensboro. The courthouse and every other building were razed to the ground. Thirty white people were killed and twice that number were wounded.

The Greene Countians quickly built several stockades and forts along the Oconee River. Settlers were careful about travel, and kept a continual watch for native visitors.

The difference between this and the wars which Charles had endured before, was the absence of a central force motivating the Creek warriors. No English or French commander was arming and encouraging them. No one was offering to buy scalps.

These Indians came out of anger and vengeance. It took several offenses for a sufficient number of them to be motivated to take the War Path.

Usually, it was only a small group of men from one village that came seeking revenge and justice. This year it might be the warriors of Salt

Creek village. Next fall, it might be Cherokee from the mountains to the north.

War came in unpredictable spurts and from unpredictable directions. But it was just as deadly. In the periods between, life was almost normal. Farms were developed, roads were improved, and the town of Greensboro was rebuilt even finer than before.

Polly Cessna recovered well from the incident. She became one of those few people who were scalped, and lived to talk about it. The experience never dulled her enthusiasm for life. And she remained a beautiful and vivacious woman.

Samuel made certain that his wife never lacked for the newest and most stylish bonnet to make up for the luster of her hair. Polly wore Quaker-style sleeping bonnets the rest of the time.

By 1793, Charles was able to convince his brother, William, to move to Georgia and take up land that Charles had selected for him.

William Cessna had grown very discouraged in Pennsylvania. When most of the Cessna boys were moving to Bedford to establish farms, their father had talked William into staying on the farm along Muddy Run.

From the beginning, William struggled to make the farm a going enterprise. His father sought to motivate the son by withholding title to the land. He acted more as a greedy landlord than an empowering parent.

In 1779, William paid tax on the 170-acre farm along with 2 horses and 2 cattle. John Cessna Sr. had a fit that William would claim ownership.

The next two years, John declared himself as the landowner, and William paid tax only on the horses and cattle.

William's father viewed his son as being not yet mature, even though he had two children, and a wife. William could not make a decent profit-producing crop to save his soul. John Cessna was sure that his son would lose the farm to bad management. So he refused to let William take the reins.

By 1793, William and his father had their last falling out. John Cessna Sr. made out his will that Spring. In it he bypassed his son William and offered gifts to William's children, Elizabeth and John. The insult was more than the William Cessna could stand.

And his brother Charles Cessna had made his invitation to relocate one too many times.

William packed his family moved to Georgia. Charles helped his older brother find a homestead near his, and life started again.

Once out of his father's shadow, William blossomed. William and Margaret Cessna settled on land first given to Charles under Head Rights. Col. Charles Cessna watched his brother, a man who had once been a lost soul, slowly come to life. The relationship of the two brothers made a fundamental shift.

William had a deep need to find a father's approval. Unable to find it before, he now sought that approval from Charles. Charles was 15 years older than William.

The Cessna clan in Georgia began to grow in strength. Within the families of William, Charles, Samuel, and John the numbers grew quite rapidly.

Charles and Elizabeth Cessna watched cautiously as both of their daughters found husbands and married. Elizabeth married James Milligan. Rebecca wed Aaron Neel. Soon, more grandchildren were arriving at Charles' door.

The valley along Richland Creek, just above where Beaver Dam Creek joins it, and only a short way from where it joins the Oconee River, became a sort of Cessna's Row.

Charles was elected Justice of the Peace and became one of the town's elders. John served as Sheriff. Samuel and his effervescent wife were heavily involved in all of the social events.

But the Indian War was not done taking its toll on the family.

CHAPTER TWENTY-FOUR
We fight, get beaten, rise, and fight again.

This most famous quote of General Nathanael Greene during the war was made during his campaign in the Carolinas. Repeatedly he seemed to be defeated and retreated. But he persisted until he turned the tables and penned the English General Cornwallis in Yorktown.

Seems like the story of my life, thought Charles Cessna as he looked out over his new home along Richland Creek. It had seemed like a good place to *rise again.*

General Nathanael Greene and Charles Cessna were the same age and were of kindred minds in several regards.

Greene's passion for victory was not born of personal gain. He sought only the protection and security of those he loved. Charles Cessna understood this type of patriotism and cherished Greene's friendship. When Greene had offered Cessna a clean start in Georgia, it was an easy invitation to accept.

On April 19, 1785, Greene gave a party and hosted all of the former officers who had relocated to Georgia. He invited them to his home for a weeklong reunion of Officers of the Revolution. His plantation, Mulberry Grove, was about 14 miles above Savannah.

It was also about 150 miles from the home of Charles Cessna. Though that seemed a daunting trip, the monthly journeys from Bedford to Philadelphia were longer.

And General Greene's invitation sounded as though this meeting was going to be just as important as the work Charles had done in Pennsylvania's congress.

Greene hosted a loose version of General Washington's Society of Cincinnatus. This was a fellowship of Revolutionary War officers who were dedicated to guiding the nation in the right direction. Washington's plan was that the veterans of the war should decide the future of the county.

It was at this meeting when Charles began to see the importance of his role in Georgia. General Greene made him feel that his presence in the state was divine providence. Greene proved to be just as charismatic and persuasive as Ben Franklin had been. He made Charles Cessna feel as though he had found a new purpose with his move to this state.

In their conversation, Col Cessna decided that the best way he could honor his hero would be to help his county and state grow into its destiny. Finding a bold sense of purpose may seem a small thing to most men. But to a man whose entire live had just been shattered, this was a life affirming moment.

It brought him from the defeat he had experienced in Pennsylvania, into a bold and hopeful sense of purpose. General Greene trusted and respected him.

It was also at this meeting when Charles Cessna experienced General Nathanael Greene's greatest asset. Catherine Littlefield-Greene was an absolute trophy of a wife. She was the kind that enriched a man's reputation for having *won her.*

She was vivacious and charming in a way that set her aside from all other women. She was intelligent and frequently engaged in challenging conversations with the gentlemen who called on her husband.

Catie Green's most endearing trait was her absolute devotion to her husband and his career. All who met her quickly fell under her spell. When General Greene died at Mulberry Grove, on 19 June 1786, Caty Greene continued to be a social influence over the Revolutionary Officers. She found ways to encourage them to continue her husband's visions.

It was through her connections with these men that Caty Greene would make her greatest contribution to America's history. Seeking innovative ways to make Mulberry Grove a prosperous plantation, Widow Greene engaged a 27 year old schoolteacher to solve a technical need.

Eli Whitney was serving as the tutor of her neighbor's children and impressed her with his ability to address difficult problems. Widow Greene had decided that Cotton was the most profitable crop for her plantation. Cotton promised to be an ideal cash crop for the southern states, but it was labor intensive.

It took a great many man hours to separate the sticky seeds from the fibers. Caty hired Whitney to find an easier way to perform the task. In a few weeks Whitney had envisioned and created a working cotton gin. In one day, two or three slaves could now perform the work that had previously taken 20-30 slaves a week to perform.

It proved to be a financial godsend to plantation owners.

Widow Greene's plantation had a profitable year. But the thing she and Whitney had created would have powerful long term effects on the institution of slavery.

Suddenly, every plantation owner wanted most of his land sown in cotton. Labor needs exploded. The price of slaves skyrocketed from hundreds to thousands of dollars per soul. Slaves were purchased in the north, moved to the south, and sold for huge profits.

The Widow Greene invited a number of officers-turned-planters back to Mulberry Grove to witness the invention. At her encouragement Charles Cessna joined several others in investing in Whitney's patent.

He added his $200 to the funds raised. They formed a company with the goal of starting a cotton-gin manufacturing plant in the north. Eli Whitney took the money and headed north.

Charles Cessna never saw that money again.

Whitney's cotton gin was immediately popular and in great demand. But it was also quite simple in design and easy to copy. Many plantation owners looked the contraption over closely; then went home to build their own version. Sales never reached what Whitney had hoped.

Every plantation was equipped with cotton gins, but very few of them had been purchased from the Eli Whitney Company. In just a few years, Whitney was bankrupt.

The cotton-gin investment became just another failed dream in Charles' life. And the friendship he offered the widow of his friend was not enough to keep her from losing Mulberry Grove to creditors.

Once again, his efforts to do something noble had fallen flat. Charles did gain a financial advantage from the entire Caty Greene episode.

He received two of the official versions of Eli Whitney's cotton-gin (short for cotton engine). He would use these to make a good deal of money raising small patches of cotton, and renting out the machines to neighbors as well.

Col. Cessna also found another way to make money. He had purchased several saw blades prior to coming south. He was able to use these to make a small, foot-powered sawmill and carpenter shop.

By training Rube in carpentry skills, Charles was able to produce decent quality furniture which he could sell to his neighbors. The furniture made Elizabeth's life more comfortable. There were no manufacturing plants in the South. So a small shops like this were doing a brisk business.

The entire system was ingenious.

A large pine spar was wedged in the rafters over the saw table, with a chain hanging from the end. When you pulled down on the chain, the spring of the beam pulled right back up again, with considerable force.

By bolting the saw blade at the end of the chain, and attaching a foot lever to the bottom of the blade, you could create an efficient up-and-down sawing-motion.

The operator stepped on the foot lever, pulling the saw blade down. The spring in the beam pulled the blade back up. The cutting happens on the upward slide of the blade. This made it possible for one man to split smaller logs and planks into usable boards and spindles.

A smaller blade worked to provide more skilled cuts. This could produce decorative trims to adorn their simple houses. While the entire shop was not enough to produce mass quantities of lumber, what it did produce was useful to a skilled carpenter.

Charles Cessna owned 300 acres of old-growth Oak and Hickory trees. This specialized sawmill converted that timber into valuable forms of furniture-grade lumber.

Rube became quite skilled at earning a profit for the Cessna family.

CHAPTER TWENTY-FIVE
Catherine

In Georgia as in Pennsylvania, Charles Cessna had a reputation for being able to acquire and keep coins.

Although he did not consider himself wealthy, many others did. In just a few years he was able to exceed the net worth he had lost in Pennsylvania. He was beginning to feel secure again. He could even lavish some of life's luxuries on his wife.

Charles had built his wife a replica of the home she had designed in Cumberland Valley Township. Using his carpenter shop, he created a house, not a log cabin.

Charles made one concession to the southern clime: it had large heavy double doors on both sides of the middle hall. This allowed a cooling breeze to blow right through the center of the home.

Over time, he had the interior walls plastered and whitewashed. And Elizabeth brightened the outside with garishly painted trim. Elizabeth began to accumulate European furniture and fabrics through the port of Savannah. Some of them she bought. And some of them she had Rube recreate for her.

Elizabeth Cessna became a prominent female voice in Greene County, just as she had once been in Bedford County. Mrs. Cessna started with her favorite pastime: organizing a weekly market for the women to swap surplus from their kitchen gardens.

She was also a key voice in the groups which held formal dances, organized community celebrations, and made things happen at the church.

Despite his brother's tutoring, William Cessna struggled. In August of 1794 he did what his brother, Charles, considered unthinkable. He and Margaret sold 62 acres of river bottom land on the Oconee for just £20.

Charles was stunned at the cheap price, and angry that his brother sold land when he should be accumulating it. Eight shillings an acre was like giving it away again. The brothers had extremely unpleasant words over the transaction. For many months it was difficult for them to be together.

What Charles did not know at that time, was that William's wife, Margaret, was failing in health. Her failing health required that William spend less time farming, and more time caring for her.

And he needed money for medicine.

Margaret Williamson-Cessna died less than a year after they sold the 62 acres.

Try as he might, Charles Cessna could just not keep life from bringing unexpected and difficult problems. He longed for a period in his life when things might be peaceful.

Greene County, Georgia needed some minds with civic responsibility. Charles Cessna accepted the position as Justice of the Peace only to find himself swamped each week by appeals to straighten out land titles.

He served as Justice from 1792 through 1798. And although he made an earnest effort to be fair and just in his rulings, he was making as many enemies as he was friends.

Land conflicts were plentiful. Corruption was so rampant among public officials that in the minds of most people, any official who decided against you had to be corrupt.

Charles was one of the few who earned "an honest reputation," but he also caught lots of criticism. It did not help that Cessna had confrontations with several of the more notorious public figures of Greene County.

Col. Elijah Clarke had signed a vast number of affidavits for war veterans seeking land grants. Hearing about land disputes as a Justice of the Peace, Charles became aware of several suspicious facts.

First was that Col. Elijah Clarke had issued certificates for far more soldiers than he could possibly have commanded during the war. The supposed number of his former officers and men rivaled the size of George Washington's entire Continental Army.

When Judge Cessna ruled against one of Col. Clarke's certificates of service, his court was visited by a furious Elijah Clarke. The outrageous Clarke made loud and spurious accusations about the court's wisdom and honesty.

Clarke was attempting to bully the justices into showing favor to anyone using his name as a reference. Col. Clarke certainly believed in grabbing as much power as was possible. Judge Cessna was wise enough not to get pulled into that power struggle.

But Charles Cessna had good reason to stand in opposition to Col. Clarke.

Elijah Clarke and Jonas Fauche were two of the Greene Countians most involved in the fraudulent Yazoo Land Deal. This was the cause of many of the court's problems.

State legislators had been bribed to allow a blatant land-grabbing scheme. When confronted by a Greensboro leader, Jonas Fauche challenged his accuser to a duel and killed him in front of the courthouse.

Elijah Clarke had been a distinguished patriot and soldier during the revolution. Now he was one of many dishonest men who were scurrying to get rich from land deals. Clarke had been seduced into seeking his own fortune.

In 1794, Clarke organized a large party of militia and moved across the Oconee River onto Creek land. Erecting a fort, he declared that he was president of his own nation state, calling it the Trans-Oconee Republic.

The U.S. Congress was furious. It ordered him to be arrested and tried for treason. The Creek Indians were also furious and just when it seemed that peace was about to take root, they returned the war path.

Charles Cessna's daughter, Catherine, became the victim of Indian reprisals against Col. Elijah Clarke's land-grabbing actions.

In September of 1794, Charles was in town with his youngest daughter. At nineteen, Catherine was a delight to him. When court business kept Charles longer than her patience allowed, he gave her permission to go home without him.

He assigned South America, their slave girl who was barely 20, to see her safely home.

Less than a mile out of town, the girls met five Creek warriors who had determined to make one last raid of revenge. Finding the girls alone on the road, they struck.

The following report was taken in deposition and sent to the U.S. Congress as part of the accounts of Indian Affairs in Georgia.

The year and day hereafter specified, came before me, Messrs, John Mikal, a wagon-man and Davis Harrison, of aforesaid State and county, and, after being duly sworn, declareth, that, on the 30ᵗʰ of September 1794, they both were near fort Fidius, where a young lady of the name of Catharine Cessna, had been just shot down, and, on examination, found a shot gun wound through her body, of which wound she died, and had been scalped; they also declare having seen a negro wench, which had received two gunshot wounds, was scalped, but had yet life in her, that, by every circumstance, they have reason to believe these horrid murders were committed by Indians; that they have heard the negro wench declare she saw five Indians, and that she was thus barbarously treated by them. The aforesaid deponents further say nothing. September 30, 1794.

Greensboro immediately mounted a posse to find the murderers. Seventeen Creeks would forfeit their lives before justice had been served.

The attack on Polly Cessna had been the opening act of this war. Now the murder of Catherine Cessna would be the last tragedy at the hands of the red man.

But Charles and Elizabeth found little solace in the peace which followed.

Catherine had been the baby of their family. Charles and Elizabeth had a special attachment to their youngest child. She doted on them as much as they doted on her. The joy she had brought to them turned into a bitter wound.

Elizabeth was the love of Charles Cessna's life. She was his truest partner in every part of his life. She was the angel who had always been his encouragement.

But with this last blow, Elizabeth slipped into her own deep depression. Her optimistic outlook faded. Her strength began to fail.

Elizabeth Cessna developed pneumonia during the winter of 1795. It was probably due to the fact that she stopped being active. His wife began to neglect her chores, and stop dreaming of new ways to improve their life. She spent long hours in front of the fire. Each day her lungs were filled with smoke instead of fresh air.

Some days Elizabeth never left her bed clothes, and let her slaves manage everything. Elizabeth left Charles' side forever in the midst of a cold February storm. She was 50 years old.

CHAPTER TWENTY-SIX
"Aren't You That Man?"

Without Elizabeth, Charles Cessna seemed at a loss for direction. His responsibilities with the court kept him from retreating to the home and becoming a depressed shell of a man.

His life kept busy, but his heart was not in it. The enthusiasm for building his community had left him at the same time as his wife's departure.

His children could see the deep emptiness which filled him. He needed a new purpose, a new challenge. The next tragedy to befall him would push him towards that new purpose.

His son Samuel, died of an unexplained fever in May of 1797. Samuel left Polly with three young children. The hardest part of this blow was not just losing his son. Charles felt completely helpless to help Polly and the children. Polly had an independent mind and her own ambitions for the future. Her plans drifted far from those of her father in law.

Charles had lost more than just a son. He had lost a daughter in law and three grandchildren.

Hardly had he worked through the grief when a still another heartache hit him.

In the spring of 1799, Charles found himself under suspicion again. Once again he was being accused of a crime.

Having taken depositions for a land case that came to the Grand Jury, Charles was accused of corruption.

One of the deponents later confessed to making perjured statements to Cessna. But it appeared to many that Charles had taken money, and knowingly accepted false testimony.

In the midst of the gossip and public debate, his past came back to bite him.

"Aren't you that man who was charged with forgery and perjury back in Bedford county?" said one of the injured parties. He asked the question in the middle of a court session.

The story of Charles' mistakes as a purchasing commissioner had never been spoken of in public. But the back room gossips had never let it die. There were other people who had made the move from Pennsylvania. They remembered and sometimes shared the stories of the Congressman who was kicked out in disgrace.

Now those charges were brought out to the public. It was a clear effort to win their case by attacking the judge.

"You are he! How did you get to be a judge? Is this whole county corrupt?"

The other members of the Grand Jury were quick to defend Charles Cessna's honesty. They investigated and made public statements in his defense.

When the criticism of the injured parties became too vocal, the Grand Jury of Greene County made an unprecedented move. They published an open letter defending Charles Cessna in the Augusta, Georgia newspaper.

Agustta, GA 1799

In response to allegations of improprieties at a recent Grand Jury Inquest in Greene County; the members of that Grand Jury are publishing the following open letter:

"We do certify that we presided as members of the last grand jury for the county aforsaid; and beg leave to submit our reasons to the public for not signing the presentments.

The implications against E. Park and therein mentioned, we concieve to be wrong. It appeared that James Bilbo, (one of the informers) in the first place made oath before Wm. Fitzpatric, Esq, that the report against said Park, respecting land grants etc, was false and erronious; and he believed were only raised to injure said Park's reputation. The said Bilbo, it also appears, was sworn afterwards by Davis Gresham, Esq, quite to the contrary of what he had sworn before; and then after that declared to the court that he knew nothing about the business and begged for mercy—that he perjured himself.

It appeared that William Carrick had sworn before Gresham, Esq about bank bills, which he said major Collier had told him about---it also appeared that the said Carrick had made oath before Charles Cessna that he was forced and seduced to swear what he did before Davis.

Gresham, Esq. and after making his counter-affidavit, run away for fear of the consequences. If Mr. Cessna did do wrong, it does not appear so; from the strictest enquire, we concieve his conduct therefore ought not to be implicated in the presentment.

The information of Mr. Hays and Mr. Jenkinson the occasion, was also nothing more than hear-say, (and that from trifling authority) we therefore conceive they ought not to carry any importation. We do further certify that there was no evidence on the occasion, nor no circumstances but *one; and that was Mr. Hay's testimony; which in fact was nothing more than hear-say; and the whole of the business appeared to us; to be nothing more than a party quarrel or dispute between the Greshams and Parks — and that we conceive the grand jury ought not to have had any thing to do with it.*

We conceive, and we are supported by the judge's charge, in saying, the reputation of no person ought to be held up to public view, from ambition or design -- sad when presentments are made, unsupported by truth -- they lose their force. In discharge of the duties we owe to God and man, and in dicharge of our oaths, as grand jurors, to present all things in its true light, that are given in charge...we do therefore declare to the world, that we conceive the reputation of E. Park, and others, implicated in the presentements, ought not thereby to be injured, in the community. We desire that this may be published with the presentments: William Greer, foreman; Ezi Rankin, William George, Charles Cessna"

The members of the Grand Jury felt that Charles Cessna had been "played." He had been given false evidence, and when he ruled on that evidence, it appeared as though he had been "bought off."

This letter was published in an effort to un- sully his name. This letter did finally allow the dust of dissention to settle around that case. But it did not help the reputation of Judge Charles Cessna. Charles resigned from public office and retreated to his home on Richland Creek.

His self-recrimination was actually much heavier than that which he received from the community.

William Cessna was panicked by the loss of his brother's dynamic leadership. He worried that the family was being dragged into some kind of a political and financial feud.

Criticism of Charles spilled over onto every member of the family. Whenever they were in town, his brother and his children were abused by the public gossip.

Such political feuds were rife in the southern states. William confronted Charles by suggesting that his public activities were making a target of every Cessna in Greene County. He began to press for some solution.

The entire family was deeply concerned by the state Charles Cessna had slipped into. Though he was silent about his pain, it was obvious to all who saw him. The final decision was made early one morning.

Charles was wide awake, but lying perfectly still in his bed. His mind used this time to sort through the issues which troubled him most.

Today he was engaged in a session of vicious self-recrimination. He played back the deaths of Samuel, and Catherine, and Elizbeth. In each case, he cataloged for himself the many ways he should have handled things differently.

He had tried so hard to make this a better world for them. But he had failed.

Charles' son Robert presented the family with a solution. Robert Cessna had never taken much of a liking to Georgia. In truth, his heart lay back in Pennsylvania, in the pretty smile of his cousin, Elizabeth Culbertson.

As soon as he turned 18, Robert bade farewell to his parents and headed back to

Shippensburg, Pennsylvania. His mother's brother, John Culbertson, still lived on Culbertson's Row, just a few miles from the town.

Robert arrived in 1793, just as the Culbertson family was ready to make their own migration south. Robert was following his heart.

He could not marry without his parents' written permission, or until he turned 21 in 1795. But Robert Cessna was not about to leave Elizabeth Culbertson's side again.

In 1794, John Culbertson moved his family down the Ohio River. His nephew Robert tagged along. In 1795, Robert Cessna married Miss Elizabeth Culbertson on his 21st birthday.

A few weeks later, he applied for his first land warrant. It was for 200 acres along the Green River in what would become Muhlenberg County, Kentucky.

Elizabeth's parents took up the 200 acres beside Robert. Or rather, John Culbertson helped his new son in law, take up 200 acres of land next to his own.

The result was the same. Robert and Elizabeth Cessna lived next door to her parents. The homes of mother and daughter were arranged to be only a few hundred yards from each other. The ladies had soon worn a nice path between their porches.

In 1798, with his farm and family firmly established, Robert Cessna sent a letter back to Georgia. He offered promise of a fresh start. He offered it just at the time when his father and siblings needed it most.

Kentucky was opening a new section of land, and offering grants of free land to veterans of the war. They were especially anxious to get veterans and officers to fill up the new spaces. It was a repeat of the promises that had brought them to Georgia. And it offered a clean start.

By spring of 1799, a new wagon train was forming in Georgia. It was pointed towards western Kentucky.

With each mile, they moved away from Greensboro, and Charles' spirit grew lighter. It was as though a great load was being taken off of his mind, one bad memory at a time.

Still beautiful and effervescent, Samuel's widow, Polly, stayed in Georgia. She remarried to John Royston on January 6, 1803.

Samuel Cessna's children: Samuel Jr., Robert, and Elizabeth, remained and founded the branch of the family that helped build the state of Georgia.

As orphans of a Revolutionary War Veteran they were allowed to participate in land lotteries. Samuel was given a land grant in Lumpkin County, Georgia.

CHAPTER TWENTY-SEVEN
A River Journey

The one thing which always brought Charles Cessna out of his depression was having a new challenge. He needed some reason to be strong in protection of others.

Organizing the trip from Georgia proved to be just the thing to bring his spirit back to him. His mind was completely occupied with anticipating every challenge they might meet. He fell back onto the work that he knew best, figuring out how much food, equipment, and manpower this small army would need.

Charles became alive again, consumed with responsibility and the feeling that his effort was important. He was needed. He was doing important things. Though he was nearly 60 years old, he had a spring in his step and a smile on his face.

Col. Cessna thrived at meeting problems head on, and finding solutions. He felt especially satisfied when he was working for the benefit of others. And this task seemed perfect for his abilities.

It was a considerable group that Charles was asked to shepherd to the new land. Over forty souls were members of his personal party.

A partial list of those residents from Greene County, Georgia who were leaving for Kentucky included:

Col. Charles Cessna, 60 years old.

The slave, Rubicon with wife, and two
daughters.

James and Elizabeth Cessna-Milligan, and
    four children: John Cessna Milligan,
    9; Melia, 7; Melina, 4 ; and Matilda, 2.
Aaron and Rebecca Cessna-Neel with two
    children: Robert Cessna Neel, 3;
    and Thomas S. Neel, 1.
John and Margaret Cessna and their four
    sons: Charles, 10; William S., 8;
    Culbertson D., 5; and James, 2.[2]
William W. Cessna Sr., the younger brother
    of Charles was just 44 years old. His
    wife having died 3 years earlier,
    William had taken a second wife,
    Mary Robinette.
William W. Cessna Jr., was just turning 20
    and still single.
John Robinett, brother of Mary Robinett-
    Cessna also joined the party with his
    wife and four of their children: John,
    12; Thomas, 10; William C., 8; and
    Margaret, 6 months.
Between them, the Milligan, Neel and
    Robinett families had a dozen slaves.

Looking at this group of pilgrims, Charles
had to be worried. He had only eight fighting men
and nearly 1,000 miles of wilderness to cross. The
women, children, and most of the slaves required
protection instead of helping to provide it.
Charles weighed the options carefully.

---

[2] The true parents of Charles, James, William S., and Culbertson
Cessna can not be verified at the publication of this book.

CHAPTER TWENTY-EIGHT
Danger

There were almost no wagon roads available to the Cessna family.

From Agusta, Charles could follow the Middle Cherokee Path to the place where Chattanooga would one day sit along the Tennessee River. It was a small Indian village at that time.

In those early days, some men were operating ferries which would help him get across. Once across the Tennessee River, rough trading paths could lead him up to the Cumberland Plateau, and through a complex series of mountain passes. That was the long and difficult road to get into Western Kentucky.

Charles judged that route would take six to nine months, and that the traveling would be costly to his group. His only alternative provided a much faster, though considerably more risky option.

The Cherokee and Chickamauga tribes had united in a national government. They bypassed the state governments and were dealing directly with the U.S. Congress for a peaceful coexistence.

This meant that in 1799, the Americans were at peace with the many tribes and villages scattered along the Tennessee River. There were still some villages in which whites were unwelcome. But most of the natives were at peace.

The Tennessee River was safe for settlers to travel. The same men who had built the ferries, were now building flat boats that could navigate the swift waters.

Using the river, the family could float its way to their new home. A month of easy river travel seemed much preferable to the longer route. Of course, such a journey carried its own dangers and threats.

In early April, which is late spring in Georgia, the group left Greensboro in a string of wagons. Heading west a short way, they encountered the old Ciscat-St. Augustine trail of the Chickamauga Indians.

This ancient path would lead them to the banks of the Tennessee River near the Cherokee village of Chattanooga. A community of boat builders was ready to assist people headed west.

Charles revived his past marketing strategy. Making a trip to Savannah, he purchased a good supply of French powder and lead. Gunpowder from France was known for being the most reliable and by far most powerful.

Once again, the further they got from civilization, the more valuable it would become. This cargo would triple its value by the time he got to the wilds of Kentucky.

He also brought his two Whitney cotton-gins, certain that they would produce cash in his new home. And he brought Rube's sawmill.

The Tennessee River made a perfect highway into Kentucky, flowing first south into Alabama, then moving north across Tennessee and Kentucky until it joined with the Ohio River. The deep and swift waters of the river would make travel quicker and easier. At three and a half miles per hour; it could carry them smoothly all the way to New Orleans if they wished.

But it brought a set of challenges which the Charles Cessna had never encountered before. The group made camp along the banks of the mighty river. There were hundreds of other pilgrims camped in the same area. It was a temporary city made up of boat builders and travelers.

Charles was able to negotiate for the construction of three flat boats. Thirty-five dollars each seemed a fair price. These boats were built to go in only one direction...pushed by the current downstream.

Each vessel was large enough to hold two or more families, their belongings, and four horses or cattle. But three boats were also more than his party could manage. It took a trio of strong men to steer and control each of the watercraft. Charles only had eight men in his party.

The flat boat was little more than a very large wooden tub which rode in the water, as opposed to on the water, as a raft might do. This gave it a little more control.

But with only a small sail, the boat was at the mercy of the river's currents. One man stood at the rear with a rudder. Two men stood on the roof of the cabin with long handled oars. With these, they had only a little control of whether the boat floated in the middle, or drifted to the side of the main current.

When it came time to rest at night, it took a great deal of effort to push the boat towards one shore or the other.

Col. Charles Cessna used the days of boat construction to educate himself on what lay ahead. Moving from tavern to tavern, camp to camp, he asked questions and copied maps from people who had been down the river before.

"The first thing you gotta get through is the gorge!" extolled a grizzled old river man. "It is 26 miles of the most beautiful and most dangerous river you have ever seen. After that, there ain't nothing to worry about but Injuns and pirates. Oh, and there's the snakes. Snakes is everywhere along the river."

"Why is the gorge so dangerous?" pried Charles.

"Well, you never know what is coming next. It might be trees hidden just under the surface, whirlpools, eddies, or shoals. And there is one huge rock right in the middle that the river likes to throw boats on.

"You have to get past Tumbling Shoals, The Holston Rock, The Kettle, The Suck Shoals, Deadman's Eddy, the Pot, The Skillet, the Pan, and finally the ten-mile Narrows. But the worst one is that whirlpool at the mouth of Suck Creek. She's a widow maker!"

Charles spent several hours with this man. He was gaining an education in how to manage or avoid all of these obstacles.

"Ole Pete" had some good advice on how to avoid, or pay bribes to, the Indian towns that lay below the gorge as well. From him, Charles was able to create a crude map of the trip ahead of them.

There were no signposts; only descriptions of landmarks at the mouth of every creek or stream joining the Tennessee River. The map he created listed no fewer than 35 noteworthy tributaries they would have to pass before they came to the flats near Cadiz, Kentucky.

The task began to seem daunting to Col Charles. The dangers began to nag in his soul.

In mid-June 1799, the group was ready to begin its float. They hoped to complete the trip and be at their new home in Kentucky by early August. This would give them time to secure their homestead and get cabins built before winter.

Charles, John, and the slave Rube would take the first boat. William Cessna and John Robinett would crew the middle boat.

James Milligan, William Cessna Jr., and Aaron Neel would crew the last boat in the flotilla. It carried the horses belonging to the entire group. All three boats were loaded to capacity and rode heavy in the current.

Charles had carefully planned everything they could need, including things to sell or trade along the way. The group seemed well prepared for the journey ahead. Every member of the group had great confidence in Charles' leadership.

Their first loss happened barely ten miles from the start. One of Milligan's slave girls had been leaning far over the side to fill a water bucket.

At that moment, the boat ran over a large, submerged tree, causing it to pitch suddenly to the right. The girl lost her balance and was flipped into the current.

Unable to swim, she sank immediately and disappeared. James jumped in the water and waited to grab her when she surfaced. But she never did.

They guessed that her clothing had been caught on part of the tree, and it prevented her from coming up. The event was a sobering blow to the group. In the blink of an eye she was gone! The children were all crying.

Charles took the tragedy to heart. He began to shout cautions to various members of the party from the time they shoved off in the morning, until the hour they lay down at night.

Because each of the boats was short on manpower, most of the younger children were placed in the middle boat. Mary Robinett-Cessna was assigned to watch over them.

The whirlpool at Suck Creek nearly cost them dearly when the middle boat was caught in the swirl. Quick thinking by John got that boat tied to the other two. As the current pushed these two boats down and past the pool, they were able to drag the third boat away from the vortex.

But it had taken several hard and frantic minutes to make the rescue happen. Charles Cessna had been caught between the bulkhead and the rope as it was pulled taut.

With the weight of two boats pressing on his chest he was unable to breathe for a few moments, and he passed out. The current made a sudden turn in the boat and the rope came free. Charles collapsed on the deck.

He was left with a deep burn across his chest. And, though he would not tell his fellow travelers, he was certain it had broken at least one rib.

Beaching the crafts on an island, John Cessna declared that the group would rest for two days. No one made any objections. The group needed to rest. But more than that, they needed time for their experiences to harden into an education of life on the river.

Every adult member of the group was sobered by these early days of the river journey.

The water was so serene and peaceful. But it could turn deadly without warning.

Many of the group thought of turning back. But it seemed impossible to make a safe trip back up the river. There was no turning back. And there was no telling what this trip might cost them before they reached the end.

Charles became obsessed with the safety of his party. He spent every minute with eyes trained on the river ahead. He soon taught himself the skill of reading what was beneath the surface of the water, by the ripples on top.

But he kept so much energy focused on the river that he began to miss other things. It was impossible for him to man any of the oars or the rudder. He was in constant pain from the broken rib. This left only one boat with a full crew of three men to steer it.

Without Charles noticing, the family became more careless about where the children played on the boat. Some of them began to play on top of the cabin. There was more open and flat space up there.

Inside the boat was so crowded that it was difficult to move around, let alone sit on the floor and play. But on top of the cabin, there were no rails to prevent them from wandering off the edge.

In the hot weeks of early summer, it was not unusual for the party to be caught in a sudden and violent thunderstorm. It created tense moments as the little ones were hurried into shelter. The men pushed frantically against the oars to find a safe place to beach the boat.

Wet and frustrated, the men waited for river to become placid again. The trip was far from easy, and far from safe.

They had been warned about Indians, and pirates, and snakes. Most of the animal life gave the party a wide birth. Deer were too frightened of humans to allow themselves to be seen for more than a brief moment.

Buffalo and bear were more curious. They could sometimes be seen silently watching the travelers from the shore. On young forest bison sacrificed himself to provide the party with a feast and fresh meat for a week.

Snakes were another matter.

It was almost a daily experience for one of the boats to pass under a large tree and have a snake drop into it. The excitement was instantaneous and very distracting for the men struggling to keep the boat on the right course.

Elizabeth Milligan became quite accomplished at dashing forward, grabbing the snake by the tail, and cracking it like a whip. The loud crack was the breaking of its neck, signaling its instant death.

Snakes were also a common hazard when they camped at night. So the women and children mostly spent the nights in the same uncomfortable wooden box that floated them down the river. Needing a break, the men slept on firm ground around a fire.

CHAPTER TWENTY-NINE
Disaster

July 13 started as a bright and beautiful day. It was destined to end in overwhelming grief.

The party had made it through the Great Gorge, and past the long section of river known as Muscle Shoals. Instead of sand bars, the river held countless shallows with crushed shells for a bottom.

The party had made it past the Lower Chickamauga villages and even the notorious Crow Town, without much incident to speak of.

At Crow Town, two warriors paddled their canoe out to meet them. They demanded payment for traveling through their lands. Col. Cessna paid them without hesitation.

At some point, Charles became aware that they were moving increasingly towards the north. The river wound back and forth on itself, so it was difficult to tell your overall direction. But most mornings found the sun coming up off of the right bank.

Col. Charles announced to the group that they were back in Tennessee Territory and that the worst of the river obstacles were behind them. This was the first day that he was able to breathe more easily and not attend so passionately to the group's safety.

Even the river seemed to be in a more pleasant mood that day. The current was flowing strong and steady with few interruptions to its surface. But something lay hidden beneath its placid surface that none of them could have anticipated.

Several years earlier, a 50-foot pine had been ripped from its place along the riverbank. It had begun a long, slow journey towards the sea.

Passing through the Gorge and the shoals, most of its branches and length had been ripped away. As the months and weeks went by, it became more waterlogged and sank deeper and deeper from sight. But it still had some buoyancy.

In late spring, the 25-foot pine spar had found a temporary home. It's roots had become entangled with another submerged tree, attaching itself to the river's bottom.

The pressure of the current gradually wedged it in an unusual position. It was pointing from the river's bed towards the sky at a 45-degree angle. It was pointing upstream.

At the current water level, it was bobbing up and down, about six inches below the surface. The weight of the water would push the upper end of the spar down about three feet, then it would spring back up with a heavy thrust.

In a few more weeks, the old pine would have become more waterlogged and either lost the strength of its spring, or broken free and floated further down river. But today, it was doing a nice little dance, up and down, just below the water's skin.

The first and third boats were drifting to the right of center stream. The middle boat was riding more to the left. With no obvious obstructions, the laxness in their formation did not seem to be a problem.

Mary Robinett-Cessna was playing with several of the children on top of the cabin in the middle boat. Her husband William was manning the rudder in the back. John Cessna, was standing above the group alternating between pushing on the right or left oar. This is why the boat was drifting that day. One man was trying to manage both oars.

Children were playing on the deck where John needed to stand when he pushed on the right oar. It all seemed harmless enough, and he could get them to move if he really needed to work the oar harder.

The front right corner of the middle barge struck when the pine spar as it was at its lowest point in the dance. The boat shuddered noticeably and the eyes of every adult widened.

Then came its upward thrust. The boat was raised on that corner more than two foot, causing the deck to suddenly tilt. With one corner stopped, but the other three still being pushed by the current, the boat made a sudden and dramatic spin.

The children had been standing in a circle on the roof, playing a game. It required them to hold hands and move in a ring around Mary. When the boat shifted, the group was thrown to their knees.

Three of the little ones did not fall down, but forward.

John's three-year-old son James, and his two cousins, Melinda, and Matilda Milligan (ages 4 & 2) simply ran off the edge of the roof into the river. They had been pushed by the momentum of the crash.

Mary shrieked in terror. Every man on the river turned in time to see her throw herself into the river after the children. It was not a dive. It was simply a leap of desperation. She was not able to reach any of the children.

John released the oars. Grabbing those children who remained on the roof, he dropped them quickly into the forward hold.

William abandoned the rudder and began to look for something he could throw to his wife to keep her afloat.

Young James was close enough that William could pluck him from the water. Intermittent screams came from the girls as they bobbed to the surface trying to keep their heads above a certain death.

None of the remaining trio could swim. Neither could William. The boat began to spin out of control pushing it further away from the strugglers.

From the last boat, James Milligan dove into the dark water and began to push through the current towards his daughters. Though he was a strong swimmer, he was at least 25 yards away.

With him not at the rudder, his boat also began to drift out of control. Far ahead, Charles could do nothing but watch in helpless horror.

Milligan reached his daughters and pulled them to the shallows. Mary was lost to the swift current, and disappeared from sight.

The tragedy seemed too great to bear. It took eight hours of searching the river's edge to find Mary's body and return her to the hastily erected camp.

Heavy despair settled onto the group. Charles sank into deep mournful sobs. Some thought he was broken by the loss of his daughter-in-law.

But his heart was crushed by the weight of having failed all those he loved. He had relaxed his guard for just a moment, and a mistake was made.

The middle boat had drifted into danger, but more than that, it had drifted just out of range for the other boats to provide the assistance it needed.

A grave was completed before dark. And the family settled in for a sullen and quiet night.

William began to act irrationally. He was in a rage. This was the second time he had lost a wife, in just 5 years. No one knew how to console him. Everyone was afraid of his rage.

In the early morning hours, William's only male slave decided to run for freedom. His master's anger frightened him. And he correctly guessed that no one in the party had any heart to chase after him.

The next morning, no one had enough spirit to restart the journey. William was beside himself with grief. He began to say that this was as far as he could go. He and John Robinett discussed making this place the end of the journey. They could start homesteads here.

Charles argued with them that this land still belonged to the Cherokee and they would be seen as trespassers.

About 10 o'clock, another floating party happened to pass them. After exchanging shouts, the group learned of the Cessna party's tragedy. They stopped to provide support.

The women of the group quickly took the children in tow and made sure they were attended to. A hearty and warm meal was prepared for the entire group.

The second group had also managed to kill a buffalo the day before. Now they roasted a good portion of the meat.

But the greatest warmth came from not being alone any longer. An amazing amount of strength and encouragement came from the spirit of new people. They were eager to press on.

The parties merged. The Hill party and the Cessna party became one. Charles was released of being solely responsible for everything. With extra men, the parties redistributed personnel and every boat was properly manned.

Children were portioned between the boats so no one group was overwhelmed with watching them.

Warm friendships were formed as the two groups became one. Charles began to allow hopeful thoughts to filter into his mind again.

John Cessna was the last of the Cessna party to purchase the family's fresh start with his life. It was senseless and a terrible waste.

After crossing into Kentucky the group began to feel safer, and relaxed their cautions. While many tribes used this territory for hunting, there were no Indian villages in the Kentucky lands.

John was gathering dead-fall branches to burn in the evening fire. He managed to startle a large water moccasin by bending down to pick up kindling. The five foot snake struck him in the right side of his neck causing him to drop to his knees in shock.

His sudden drop moved him closer instead of away, and the snake hit him again. This time it struck in the cheek, just below his eye.

The poison was enough to provide a quick but very painful death. Charles Cessna held his son as the venom took his life.

Now it was Charles' turn to become irrational. He went into a blind rage at the foolishness of the accident. His two sons-in-law had to restrain him from self harm.

It was all too much for Col. Cessna. His confidence had vanished. This journey had been his greatest effort at planning and executing a mission. But the price was too great. Every lost life haunted him as a personal failure.

With less than a hundred miles left to travel, he could not bring himself to lead any longer. He simply retreated into the bed and would not come out.

Then an amazing thing happened.

William, who had never shown much leadership or ambition, stepped into the role of the group's captain. In his brother's absence, he began to give gentle commands about what needed to be done, assigning tasks that employed everyone and took their minds off the grief.

Sitting patiently beside his brother, William reminded the Colonel that many lives could still be lost if they delayed or gave up. In a gentle but firm voice, William commanded Charles to leave his bed and pack it for the day. And whenever Charles seemed lost about what to do, William would quietly remind him of the task he should assume.

William was assuming his brother's leadership role. It was working.

Charles had led the group with courage and heroic love. Now he was incapacitated by grief and depression. William was leading the group by imitating his brother's style. In a very strange way, Charles was still leading.

The Hill/Cessna party reached the landings near Cadiz, Kentucky in late August. It had four fewer souls than when it had started. But with the new land, came the excitement of a new beginning.

Hope returned.

CHAPTER THIRTY
A letter

The trip from the river to their new homes was much easier than they had anticipated. With the increased number of travelers, a rough freight service had begun.

It was just a two day journey by wagon to move all of the people and belongings to their new home.

Charles had been correct in his assessment of the value of the black powder. By selling the boats, and one small keg of gunpowder, the entire expense of the moving all six families was reimbursed to him. The boats would soon be reloaded with wheat, corn, tobacco, and hogs by the local farmers and floated down to New Orleans.

A welcoming party greeted them.

Robert Cessna and a large delegation of the Culbertson family met them at their new home sites. A warm family reunion was held.

Their leader, John Culbertson, had already selected a promising section of land for each of them. The transition was the easiest that Charles had ever made in his life.

A very lush region of forest and meadow lay alongside the Cyprus Creek, just a few miles from the new village of Greenville.

With the creek at its back, Charles' new farm showed exciting potential. And with all of the men working together, homes were erected with amazing speed.

John Culbertson was holding something precious for their arrival. He had brought with him a letter from Charles Cessna, Jr.

The son had written letters to his mother through the years, but had never addressed one to his father, until now.

Charles carried it in his pocket for many days before he found the courage, and the privacy to read it. The gulf between father and son was now 16 years long. It was not based on anger, but on each other's shame at the events which destroyed the father's life.

Two proud men simply did not know how to talk to the other. So one thing forever separated them. There was no bitterness, just embarrassment at the level which made it difficult to address each other.

Dearest Father,

From the reports which Mother sent, it would appear that the challenges of this life have not grown any easier for you. My heart breaks also at the loss of Catherine. And I continue to send my love and pride in your support.

You know that I have two sons. James was born in 1788 and William Franklin was born in 1790.

My daughters, Rachael, Rebecca, and Maria, are a constant delight to my heart. They would adore showing off their talents and charms to entertain you.

I have prospered well in your absence. In '94 Pennsylvania allowed a new round of land grants for veterans and their children. They were really just trying to fill up all the unsettled corners of Bedford County.

I have improved and claimed a right nice farm of 400 acres. It is about 11 miles northwest of the town.

It has a nice stream right down the middle. And I am able to bring in significant amounts of corn and wheat each season, not to mention three cuttings of hay in most years.

The Cessna farm has more than enough room for Charles Sr. and Charles Jr. if you should ever decide to return to these lovely coves. I would be most honored if you should come and share this bounty with me, just as you once shared yours with myself.

I wish I could say that the political climate of our little county has changed for the better, but it has not. Each election seems to divide the people more deeply and the spirit of politicking gets meaner by the year.

Uncle John has been bitten hard several times. If you will allow me, I would like to share one example of which I was most proud of him.

Col. George Woods and his son continue to dominate the local scene and tend to bully their way around. Both are firm in the camp of the Federalists.

Uncle John and many others are active in the Democratic Republic Society which meets at the tavern of Cornelius McCoy. The election of 1786 was a significant showdown for these two groups. Woods and James Martin were running for the office of Representative. They took some mighty good licks at each other, and their confederates were most active in the fight as well.

After the election, a great furor about fraud erupted and Philadelphia held an investigation. Uncle John was called to testify in person.

I am not sure what all occurred, but John was claiming that a number of ballots had been destroyed illegally. He claimed that some voters were turned away because they forgot to bring their loyalty certificates to the ballot. It also seems that the votes of the entire Standing Rock township were thrown away because they arrived too late.

Whatever the details, Uncle John was quite furious that it was only those voters in support of James Martin who were denied. So he went to Philadelphia to get the election taken away from Woods and given to Martin.

As you can imagine, Woods was not too happy about this. And what he did next is one of the most despicable things I have ever heard about him.

You knew that Aunt Sarah had died and Uncle John remarried to Elizabeth Hall. What is not spoken of much is that Elizabeth was a teenage girl whom John had hired to care for Aunt Sarah in her ailing days. John married her just three weeks after Sarah died, and their first son was born only seven months later.

I have never asked him why, but he named the boy Charles. I suppose it to be in your honor.

George Woods hatched a dastardly plan to embarrass Uncle John. He arranged for some of his confederates to have Elizabeth arrested and charged with Fornication and Bastardy.

Poor Elizabeth was dragged before the judge and shamed quite pitiably. I am told that the men outside the courthouse got in such an argument that fisticuffs broke out. I witnessed that Sheriff McGaughey, one of Wood's own men, was sporting a black eye for several days. Elizabeth was found guilty and fined £10. The entire performance was just to humiliate her and sully Uncle John's reputation.

What happened next still has me bristling with pride. Uncle John caught Col. Woods in the street in front of the courthouse. They went at each other for near 40 minutes. How my uncle kept from striking him or challenging him to a duel is beyond me.

But John's words were the most carefully chosen of any I have ever heard. He completely sliced Mr. Wood's character apart like he was butchering a hog. I do believe my uncle's restraint was because he knew that it was his own sin which had hurt Elizabeth more than Mr. Woods'.

The entire county was angered by the proceedings. I can tell you with pride that Mr. Woods did not win his next election. But Uncle John was elected as Justice of the Peace for the township and has served as such since then. His honesty is much praised in this county.

I want to say, father, that your own reputation in this region is much more apprized than you might think. I have considerable pride when people tell me how fondly they remember Col. Cessna's service during the war. You have many friends and admirers here. You are honored in my life and home.

Your loving son, Charles.

CHAPTER THIRTY-ONE
Kentucky

The reception in Kentucky was a warm one. Robert Cessna and John Culbertson had arranged temporary shelters and a large meal.

A new spirit of enthusiasm took hold of the group of weary travelers. A new beginning is always exciting. Here was an opportunity to build. They needed to create new homes, new farms, new friendships, and an entirely new community.

Charles had done this twice before. The first time was in organizing Bedford county in Pennsylvania. The second was in the formation of Greene county, Georgia. And now this opportunity lay before him once again.

Muhlenberg county had formed in 1798 by taking large section of the old military reserve from Christian and Logan Counties. Everything was starting fresh. It was thrilling to be there at the very beginning.

Charles Cessna, however, could not get excited. He would never be fully invested in this home in Kentucky. For some reason it felt foreign to him. Kentucky would never feel like home.

His daughters Elizabeth and Rebecca guessed that he was having much difficulty in dealing with the losses of their journey. His mood looked all too familiar to them.

As small children they had watched their mother carefully as she tended the emotional wounds of this man they loved. Every loss of life during the war had been a personal blow to him.

There had been times when Charles Cessna fell into his chair, filled with desperation. Their mother knew just how to encourage him. Somehow, she managed to put his strength back into the tasks which faced him.

Elizabeth Culbertson and Charles Cessna had always been more than business partners, or even husband and wife. They dreamed each other's dreams. Together, they had faced every form of dragon which had threatened their family.

Elizabeth had held him together in Bedford, and again in Georgia. But she was no longer by his side. The loss seemed insurmountable for Charles Cessna.

Neither his daughters nor his grandchildren seemed enough to make the old man laugh. Charles Cessna was feeling every one of his sixty years. He was weary of heart and body.

There was, however, one way Charles could help his clan. He could use the money he and Elizabeth had saved over the years to give them a good start.

His son, Robert, and his brother-in-law, John Culbertson, had a promising section of land all picked out for the new group. It was on Cypress Creek, near to where it emptied into the Green River.

Their own homesteads were just five miles east, at the wide valley where Nelson Creek joined the same river. The community of Central City would soon grow up in a place halfway between the groups.

The family staked out three separate farms. Charles Cessna, the Neel family, and the Widow of John Cessna built homes on one. William Cessna and his brother-in-law, John Robinett built their homes on the second. James and Elizabeth Milligan began a smaller farm tucked neatly between the other two.

After a year of building houses, barns, paddocks, and fields, the family was ready to apply for ownership.

That was the proper way to do things in Kentucky. Find an empty piece of land. Mark it out. Build a cabin and start improving the property. When it has been developed enough, you could travel to the land office and formalize your claim.

On the 23rd day of March in 1801, Charles Cessna paid the appropriate fees and made a claim for 200 acres on the waters of Cypress Creek. He returned on July 27th and filed a second claim for 200 acres adjacent to the first. The land registrar then requested the state surveyor to make an official map of the property.

Although Charles remained in his deep depression, the others in the group kept pressing until all of this was done. By the time he was ready to make the July trip to the land office, Charles Cessna admitted that his departed bride would have been proud of it all.

The family was flourishing.

And the Cessna family began to get involved in the development of the county. In the early days, when the number of people was small, everyone was needed.

James Milligan, Aaron Neel, and William Cessna served on the first Grand Juries. This body made decisions about prosecuting crimes. But more importantly, it was the Grand Jury and the Court of Common Pleas which made all decisions about how tax monies would be spent to develop roads and other infrastructure.

Robert Cessna was selected by the Governor to be the first Justice of the Peace for the county. Col. Charles Cessna had a long history of civic service in the courts. His name was suggested to the governor as the first County Coroner.

Because of his age, and another factor which the family was unaware of, John Culbertson was chosen over Charles Cessna. The old man did not mind a bit. His heart was not in the political competition which was developing with the new county.

The Grand Jury named William Cessna to be one of the Road Commissioners. Early court records list a number of times he was assigned to lay out the roads connecting remote families to several villages which were springing up around the county.

The Cessna Family had arrived in Kentucky. The men of the family could be found in every public venue. The women of the clan helped form weekly markets in Central City. They also encouraged some of the first religious services in the community.

Everyone was excited, except the man who had made of this all possible. Charles Cessna's heart lay in a wild forest where he had buried his son.

Kentucky just did not stir his soul.

It did not help much that the first two seasons of 1800 and 1801 failed to produce the cash crops for which the group had hoped. Clearly it was going to take some new skills to make this rocky soil produce corn and cotton.

CHAPTER THIRTY-TWO
Shadows of The Past

Life in Kentucky was hard. Entertainment was crude. Any surplus wealth was invested in building fine but isolated homes, or in acquiring more slave labor. A very rough sort of man infested the waterways of all the Kentucky rivers. Crime was much more prevalent than it had been in Georgia or Pennsylvania. Even murder of white man on white man was common.

And there was something about Kentucky which the Cessna family had been unable to foresee. The new people brought with them old grudges and feuds. A large number of the new settlers had come from south central Pennsylvania, just as had Robert Cessna and John Culbertson.

The name of Col. Charles Cessna was not unknown among those people. Not all of them had forgotten the scandal of 15 years earlier.

Rumors of the sullied reputation of Col. Cessna began to quietly circulate among the taverns and stables of the county. It was these very rumors which had blocked Charles' nomination as coroner.

On a bright Saturday morning, Elizabeth and Rebecca talked their father into accompanying them to the weekly market in Greenville. They hoped it would do the old gentleman some good to get out in public.

In Georgia, Judge Charles Cessna had been well known and respected. The happy greetings he got always seemed to boost his mood. Perhaps the same would happen for him here in Kentucky.

It did not take very long before someone recognized him. A strange voice suddenly called out to stop the group from its casual stroll through the fruits and vegetables.

"Hey! I know you from somewhere?"

Charles Cessna turned, but had absolutely no recognition of this man. Because of the prominent positions he had once held, it was not unusual for someone to recognize him, and for him not to return the favor.

"You are that Colonel who stole all the money from the militia, ain't ya? I remember you, they had to run you out of town or something like that." The man turned to the crowd and began to expound the rumors he had heard. "Or did you go to prison?"

His facts were heavily clouded by the distance and time, but he sounded like he was an expert in the matter.

"Cesny! That's it. You're Colonel Cesny!" he yelled as Charles and his daughters turned to leave the market. Then the man turned back to the listening crowd to give his manipulation of history.

Charles almost stopped and engaged the man in clarification. But he could see the man had no real interest in him personally. And he certainly had no interest in the truth.

The fellow was entirely happy to have some new bit of information which made him the center of attention. Charles Cessna meant nothing more to him than a reason to get others to listen to him.

However, several in the crowd were now staring at Charles. You could see the judgment in their eyes. Colonel and his daughters made their way back to their homes on Cypress Creek.

Charles became a recluse from that day on. It did not matter that the crowd in town quickly forgot the issue and moved on to newer gossip.

There was hardly a man among the recent immigrants who did not have some dark secret in his past. That was what new beginnings in new places were good for.

But when added to the depressed state of his mind, this new blow caused him to become even more withdrawn. His spirits plummeted. He was reluctant to even leave his home for church services.

Those who knew Charles Cessna intimately, knew that he lived a life of careful honesty. He worked hard to provide for his family, but had little personal ambitions for wealth.

If anything Charles Cessna was too generous with his assets in support of others. To his family, the unjust burden of his tarnished past seemed far too unfair a punishment.

CHAPTER THIRTY-THREE
Mississippi

It was his brother William who offered an escape from Charles' self imposed exile. The rumors about Col. Charles Cessna's past had begun to be a problem for other members of the family. The stories of his charges were now not merely tavern gossip.

When William and Robert Cessna began to run for election, the shadow of Col. Charles Cessna made its way into the political arena.

In 1801, Robert Cessna resigned his position as Justice of the Peace. The ugliness of political critics was too much for him.

William Cessna soon followed his example, and abandoned his role as Road Supervisor. Both men stepped back from public service. Their sacrifice was not lost on Charles Cessna.

It was in the Spring of 1801 that William Cessna came to visit his brother. He had an interesting bit of news.

During the Spring and Summer of 1801 the Choctaw Nation was negotiating with the United States to allow whites to settle along the Natchez Trace, and along the Mississippi River from Nachez down to Spanish Territory.

A vast new area of free land would be available as soon as the Treaty of Fort Adams was signed. But some men were not waiting for the signing. In the Fall, a group of Cessna men went south to explore what land was available.

At first, Charles Cessna argued against the journey. But his daughters insisted that the younger men needed his wise counsel if they were going to make the trip safely. It would be mid-winter before they would return.

The land in Mississippi was everything that had been promised. Thick forests of tall trees shaded a soft carpet of pine needles. An extraordinarily rich soil lay within easy reach. The Mississippi River had spent the last 10,000 years getting this bottomland ready for their plows.

The prospect was exciting. And every day they spent away from the political ugliness in Kentucky made the old man smile a bit more.

Charles Cessna, James Milligan, and Aaron Neel chose three sections of land in an area which would one day become Hinds County.

William Cessna and John Robinett pushed further to take a look at the legendary city of Natchez. They found land to their liking a short way east of town and made claims for farms for each of them. William Cessna Jr., though single, was now old enough, and a claim was started for him as well.

Farmsteads of about 200 acres were laid out and the first improvements were made. That first year they cleared some trees and fenced in a paddock. Cabins were started, but those would have to wait until the summer of 1802 to be completed.

A toehold was made in Mississippi.

Back in Kentucky, the excitement spread through the entire family. Robert Cessna listened to stories told by the group and was tempted to join them. But his wife, Elizabeth, informed him in very certain terms, that she was not about to leave her parents or her new home.

Robert Cessna and family remained in Muhlenberg County. Eventually, the political gossip faded and Robert Cessna became a noted community leader.

To Charles' great disappointment, Margaret Cessna, widow of his son, John, decided against another move. She was having a challenging time making a new life as it was.

There was still the four boys Margaret had to care for: Charles, James, Culbertson, and William. It did not seem prudent to her to carry them on another journey through the wilderness. It was the same untamed wilderness which had taken her husband from her.

Still youthful, Margaret had hopes of finding a new husband. Several promising candidates also encouraged her to remain behind. Though he would miss the excitement of his four grandson, Charles dared not discourage Margaret from pursuing her own path. It hurt deeply to lose four more grandchildren from his world.

One last member of the Cessna clan chose to remain in Kentucky.

In April of 1802, Sally Cessna married James Sharp. James Sharp was among those people from Pennsylvania who had come to Muhlenberg County.

William Cessna and the Sharp family had been close neighbors back in Letterkenny Township of Franklin County. The newly wed couple raised a large family in Muhlenberg county.

So, although, Central Kentucky proved to be just a temporary stop on the migration of Col. Charles Cessna's family. They did leave behind a strong contribution to the settlement of Central City and the county.

CHAPTER THIRTY-FOUR
Pirates!

This new migration was organized by the younger men. Charles was still consulted for advice.

Charles would provide the cash and political collateral to make the trip happen. John Robinette, James Milligan, Aaron Neel, William Cessna Sr., and Jr. would add to the number of guns and protection on the trip.

And late in the planning stages, an old friend from the river journey, John Hill, would bring his family and join the group.

The move from Pennsylvania to Georgia had been dangerous only because of the normal hazards of travel and exposure to the weather and demanding work.

The move from Georgia to Kentucky had offered all of that same danger, and much more. The Tennessee River carried the party easily and swiftly through a wilderness that was rife with Indians, bandits, pirates, and wild predators. That journey had cost lives.

Now, the trip from Kentucky to Mississippi promised to be the most threatening and difficult of all. Spain controlled all of the land west of the Mississippi. With plenty of good reason, they feared the lawless Americans who sought to ply the river for trade.

The Mississippi River had been closed for travel to all Americans for several years. The easiest route, floating down the Green River to the Ohio, then down to the Mississippi, and then south to New Orleans, was absolutely forbidden to them.

All American merchants and farmers seeking to get to the markets in New Orleans had only one option. The Natchez Trace was little more than a dirt path through the wilderness.

It had begun life as a trail cut by giant herds of buffalo when migrating between seasonal grasslands. Its entire length ran from the Ohio River near Cincinnati to the Spanish colony of Natchez on the lower Mississippi River.

The 400 miles to Natchez was easy to travel. But it was even easier to fall ambush to hostile forces.

The road was sunken from the continual passage of heavy animals, and provided a high bank on either side from which danger could suddenly appear. The narrow lane made it difficult for travelers to bunch together in a defensive formation.

The most notorious of the bandits that exacted their toll along the Natchez Trace, happened to be a past acquaintance of Col. Charles Cessna.

Samuel Mason had been a captain in both the Virginia and Pennsylvania Militias before and during the Revolution. When Washington County was formed from Bedford County, Mason served several terms as Justice of the Peace. He was well known among the political leaders of Bedford County.

The same year that Charles had moved to Georgia, Samuel Mason had moved to Kentucky. At some point he abandoned all pretext of normal life, and became a pirate and bandit.

Mason became head of the notorious band of thieves that based itself at Cave In Rock. They preyed on all boats who tried to pass by on the Ohio River below.

In the summer of 1799, a group of men from Mercer County, Kentucky, calling themselves "the Exterminators" cleaned out Cave In Rock. Mason fled to an island in the Mississippi under Spanish authority.

There he set up a highly organized business of extorting money from people traveling the river, or plundering those who resisted. When the Spanish arrested him he protested that he was an honest merchant. But when they found $7000 and 20 human scalps in his baggage they convicted him of piracy.

Mason managed to escape before they could hang him. In 1802 he was focusing his illicit business only on the travelers along The Natchez Trace.

Shortly after the Cessna party crossed into Mississippi Territory, Samuel Mason, and a party of twenty very hard-looking men surrounded and confronted them. Some of Mason's men were half breeds or renegade Indians. The members of the Cessna party were terrified.

Colonel Charles stepped forward to negotiate for the group. Usually such bandits only wanted tariff. They did not like to waste ammunition killing those they robbed.

Charles immediately recognized Samuel Mason. The elderly Colonel addressed the pirate as though he were an old friend. His fearless approach to the bandit was disarming.

"Captain Mason?" said Charles stepping forward with a large grin on his face, "Well, God be praised, that is you."

In a few moments Charles had reminded his foe of past occasions they had shared, and common causes for which they had bled. They had first met on the day following the massacre of Captain Phillips' company near Shoup's Fort.

Mason's company of Rangers had followed the War Party all the way from Fort Pitt, but arrived too late to help with anything but the burial. On that occasion, Col. Cessna had provided Mason and his men with desperately needed food and ammunition.

And throughout the War, when Mason's Rangers got close to Bedford, they knew they could find help from Col. Cessna.

Charles never forgot that the man before him was a pirate. He never underestimated the danger his family was in. And he never let up on the game he was playing.

Calling others forward, Col. Charles introduced Samuel Mason as a hero of the late war. Rather than calling him the pirate he was, Charles reminded the man of the decent community leader he had once been. The effect was disarming.

Charles even went as far as to say that he had been hoping to meet Mason on this journey. "I had heard that you were providing protection to families such as mine. These woods are full of unscrupulous characters. Would you allow me to offer a reimbursement for your protective services?"

Mason was absolutely astounded. No one had willingly offered him money before. And the thought of being addressed as a protector instead of a feared villain put him off balance.

Cessna offered a payment of $100 for safe passage through Mississippi. And he added two jugs of Kentucky Whiskey as a gratuity.

Although Mason would normally have gotten more, he accepted this gift and let the group pass. Mason declined the offer of having dinner with the Cessna party. And he even made a feeble promise to visit Charles' new home in the months ahead.

Samuel Mason, the Outlaw, did one more thing which was completely out of his character. Watching Col. Cessna with his family, he must have been touched by memories of his own family. He had lost every one of them to the war.

Pulling the old comrade aside, Mason gave Cessna a grave warning. "Natchez is not a place for a man to raise his family. It has grown plum full of undesirables." Cessna was taken aback by the man's candor.

"If you were to take my advice, let me suggest someplace else. About 40 miles before you get to Natchez, you will come to a large meadow that was burned out by a lightning fire. The sunken road opens up to a nice wide flat place for about two miles, and you will be able to see how the grass was burned last year."

Mason was obviously giving his old acquaintance something valuable. He spoke as though he were passing on a precious secret.

"If you turn straight south, you will find some mighty pretty land; beautiful meadows just ready for farming, surrounded by tall deep woods all around. And if you are smart you will build far off of any path or road. I expect the Indians ain't quite all that pacified yet."

Less than a year later, Charles heard that Captain Samuel Mason had met his end on the Mississippi, just a short way from Natchez.

His own men killed him in a fight over how their treasure was to be divided. Then, the pirates took his head to the Spanish to claim a bounty reward that had been posted up and down the river.

Charles thought it a great irony that Mason's men soon met their own demise. When they returned to the American side of the Mississippi to spend their reward, they were immediately arrested. The last of Mason's pirate band were hanged for their crimes in Greenville, Mississippi.

When the Cessna Party came to the burned meadow that Mason had told him about, Charles realized that Mason had been pointing him towards land which he had discovered for himself a year earlier. He found himself agreeing with the pirate about its attractiveness.

The party was divided at that point.

Charles, the Hills, the Milligans, and the Neels headed southeast. William Cessna, his son, and the Robinetts continued south.

Colonel Charles, James Milligan, and Aaron Neel took up farms near each other in the glades and meadows of what would become Hinds County. Milligan claimed 438 acres; Cessna claimed 271 acres; Neel claimed 300 acres; and Hill claimed 197 acres. All of these farms were in the Bayou Pierre watershed.

William Cessna, his brother-in-law, John Robinette, and his son William, Jr. traveled 40 miles further down to Natchez and settled with 320 and 280 acres, respectively. They settled in the Homochitto River watershed.

The two cotton-gins brought by Charles Cessna were divided between. And the Cessna family became cotton farmers once again.

The cotton-gins owned by Charles became the basis for the local economy. He made money by renting his machine, as well as using it for his own modest plantation.

Charles Cessna Neel arrived in late 1802 as the families were getting established. Everyone thought this child to be a good omen for this new beginning.

James Milligan Jr. joined the clan a few weeks later. Life was at last growing sweet and peaceful for Col. Charles.

Their new homes were located deep in a thick pine forest. Meadows of 3 to 10 acres were converted into isolated cotton fields. James Milligan chose to build a home on the old man's land which was large enough to include Charles. Aaron Neel, chose a farm about six miles to the west.

CHAPTER THIRTY-FIVE
Hinds County

The soil was rich beyond anything they had seen previously. The girls soon had kitchen gardens producing a wonderful variety of foods.

Charles beamed in pride because each had been taught these skills by their mother. Elizabeth Culbertson was the amazing gardener who had attracted him so many years earlier. Every time Charles sat down to a meal, it was as though Elizabeth was still with him.

The woods were full of game. The family was able to kill and feast. In the early years they even found an occasional forest buffalo. One time James Milligan brought home a bear.

The farm laid out by Colonel Charles Cessna in the pine forest of Mississippi has remained with his descendants for 200 years. Throughout the generations they have told an interesting story about those early days.

When Charles returned with the larger party to finish the claim started a year earlier, he was surprised to find it occupied. An elderly Creek man had built a small hut along the stream. He placed it at the opposite end of the meadow where Charles had started his cabin. It was a simple thing made from river cane, with mud plastered walls, and a thatched roof.

When the rest of his people sold the land to the United States and moved west, this gentle man had just stayed behind. This was the land where he had been born. His simple request was to live out his last days near the places of his most pleasant memories.

Charles Cessna insisted that the man be left alone. Though never becoming friends, the kindred souls of two old men watched each other from a thousand yards distance. Occasionally, they nodded to each other.

The ancient Creek warrior died in his sleep a year or so later. The Cessna family buried him in the same plot where their own family would rest in the decades to come.

Other souls would rest with the Cessna family as well. The slave, Rubicon, had taken a wife. They had two daughters. And when their days were full, all of them joined the family in final sleep.

The weather was mild, even if the insects were ferocious. Only one shadow crossed their first days in Mississippi. 1804 saw the arrival of another large wave of new settlers. And with the new people came smallpox.

Governor Claiborne was swift to act and initiated the first mass inoculation for the entire territory. As they were planting in the Spring, a troop of soldiers arrived at Charles Cessna's plantation. They were escorting a doctor.

While most of the frontier people were resistant to the idea of inoculation, Charles Cessna was not. He remembered the words of Ben Franklin about how such new ideas could save many lives. The offer fit well with Col. Cessna's need to keep his family from harm.

Unfortunately, the doctor arrived too late with his intervention. The fever had struck a number of the children and some adults as well.

Elizabeth Cessna-Milligan and two of her children perished before the Summer of 1804 had ended.

James Milligan was beside himself. He had lost the love of his life. He was left with six children, aged 14 through 2. And his heart was no longer in Mississippi. James Milligan and his children moved back to Muhlenberg County, Kentucky.

One more time, a piece of Charles' heart was torn from him. He watched the Milligan family leave his home. Charles Cessna was left behind, with nothing but Rubicon's family to fill his house.

In his heart, he was like that old Creek warrior. He just wanted to live out his last days in peace. He almost never went into the village of Utica. The slaves avoided going into town as well. Ruthless men were kidnapping slaves and selling them for huge prices in New Orleans.

The wagon carrying James Milligan and the children left in early October. Travel on the Natchez Trace was much safer by then. They had just been gone four days when they returned. They brought a great surprise for the old Colonel.

James Milligan had met another party of travelers on the way. He needed to show them the way to Cessna's farm.

Margaret, the widow of John Cessna, had also fallen victim to the pox. Two of her four sons had gotten it too, but they survived.

Fourteen-year-old Charles Cessna had taken his brothers William, Culbertson, and James to find their beloved grandfather. It was a 400 mile trip, but these boys were determined.

"Grandpa, they were talking about us going to live with Uncle Robert. And you know how Aunt Elizbeth is….well prickly!" Charles explained.

"Me and the boys decided we didn't want no part of living with Aunt Elizabeth. So we just lit out early one morning. I doubt that anyone is seriously gonna miss us. Anyway, that was months ago. And we are here now!"

Charles was amazed that the four youngsters had traveled so far alone. Obviously, they had received help from other travelers on the Trace. These boys definitely had the spirit of his son, John, living in their bones.

James, the youngest, was only 6. And he had just walked 400 miles to see his grandfather.

When the Census Taker came around in 1805, he found Col. Charles Cissna living with four slaves, and three boys under age 16: William, Culbertson, and James. Young Charles Cessna was working for, and living with, Aaron Neel's family just a few miles away.

The old soldier's bones were growing weary. But life seemed to be coming to that peaceful place he had longed for. To make sure it stayed peaceful, Charles Cessna avoided all political or community strife in his later days. He was sixty-five years old. The world could go on without him. He had plenty of shady places to inspect on his property.

Charles Cessna even forbade his children and grandchild from referring to him as "Judge," or "Colonel," or any of the other honorifics he had earned through the seasons of his life. He wanted no notoriety.

He had the lively spirits of four young men to entertain him. That was enough for any old soul.

Under his supervision, the labors of the boys, and that of the slaves, his plantation began to prosper. Not greatly, but not shamefully either.

CHAPTER THIRTY-SIX
The letter

In 1810, Charles finally found the courage it had taken 25 years to attain. He wrote to Charles, Jr. to explain feelings he had never before had the words express.

My darling son,
I shall never be able to convince you of my love, and the pride which rests on your memory. Though I have been remiss in my attendance of you, these have never faded in the slightest. It is my own guilt and shame which have kept me from looking into your eyes.

The accident you suffered did not cause my fall. It was my own poor judgment and choice to lie which caused my problems. I had hoped that if I was not present to cause you any further shame, you might be able to salvage the honor in your life. I have been absent not from shame of you, but for fear that my presence might bring shame on you. I see now that I have been in a prison of my own making.

I would share one gift with you. It is a lesson learned from hard choices and even more bitter loss. It is the secret to finding peace. That precious gift which eluded me has finally come to me. And when it found me, I was the most surprised of all men.

I thought if I moved away from my problems, I might find peace. I wanted so for your mother to find a happy place to shine in her glorious way. But with every move, strife and conflict followed.

Try as I might to do the best thing, the worst always found us. I have learned that running from problems does not bring you peace. I have found peace, though. It comes from love and patience. It found me when I quit searching for it. It is in knowing what few things are really important, and which of life's distractions are not. I must say, I have no idea how I found it, or if it found me, but I am grateful it has come at last.

My life has become quite simple now. I rise to greet each day and sift through the memories of people and places I love. Each evening, I tuck the sun into her glorious coverlet, knowing that I am blessed.

Your memory visits in that hour of sunset.

So my dearest son, as I ask you to forgive me my many failings, I promise to meet you again, on the other side.

Father.

CHAPTER THIRTY-SEVEN
The Horsemen

Charles sought to bring the boys up with the traditional values of gentlemen. He schooled them in the classic literature of romantic heroes ... Roland, King Arthur, Greek mythology, and of course, the Normans who conquered England. They were his personal ancestors. He told them stories about his grandfather, the French Cavalryman who had endured religious persecution.

The boys played soldier and adventurer throughout the forests of central Mississippi. Reaching their teens, the Cessna brothers became well known for wandering the countryside on horseback, searching for trouble, and damsels-in-distress. They were living an amazing life.

Their grandfather provided them with horses, guns, sabers, and all of the toys young men enjoy. Charles never understood though, why they had to run their horses at full gallop everywhere they went. Walking got you there just fine.

Days at the Cessna plantation were punctuated with stampedes of young men racing home from the woods, practicing saber duels with each other, or pushing the boundaries of common sense in one form or another. They were boys.

They were living on the edge of the wilderness, but being taught to live as aristocracy. And they had no mother figure to temper their spirits.

In short, it was chaos. Loud chaos!

Charles suspected that his sweet Elizabeth rolled over in her grave at least once every day. These young men idolized soldiering. Their grandfather was a famed veteran of many campaigns during the Revolution.

If the bragging they did to their friends was to be believed; Col. Charles Cessna had been at Valley Forge, the taking of Trenton, and the surrender at Yorktown. George Washington had been his best friend!

Of course he had done none of those things.

It is of little surprise that when rumors of another war with England began to appear in the newspapers, these boys talked of joining the fight.

Charles knew that he would not be able to hold them back. When he reached his seventy-first birthday, he realized that his days with them were ending.

Chales began to make final arrangements.

The younger Charles was given ownership of the plantation. It was not done through a will so there was nothing recorded at the County offices.

In fact, ownership of this farm would be passed from generation to generation for two hundred and twenty years.

On the 23ʳᵈ day of July in 1811, Charles Cessna did make one trip to the County Court House. He recorded an interesting bill of sale. Avoiding probate, Charles recorded that he had "sold" all of his movable property to the remaining three grandson.

William Cessna, Culbertson Cessna, and Joseph Cessna became the joint owners of the following: *one roan horse, one black mare, one sorrel colt, eighteen head of horned cattle, thirty head of hogs, all of my household furniture and farming utensels (sic).* Aaron Neel was a signing witness.

In this way, Charles Cessna passed on all of his worldly possessions before he made his farewell. The household furniture was not really so valuable. Surviving six years of three rowdy boys had left most of it scarred and damaged.

As a judge, he had seen too many families pull themselves apart fighting over their father's estate. He settled any arguments long before he lay down the final time.

CHAPTER THIRTY-EIGHT
War and Goodbye

On the 1st day of June 1812, President James Madison went to Congress with a list of grievances against Great Britain. Before he left their chambers, the Senate had declared war on England.

General William Henry Harrison immediately invaded Canada at Detroit. The United States was once again at war with the King of England.

Everyone of Charles' grandsons was passionate about going to war. But none wanted to leave their grandfather alone. Culbertson and William Cessna were the first to sign up. James and Charles (the youngest and the oldest) would remain with their grandfather.

The aged Colonel watched these two young men ride off to war on horses he had given them. He did not live long enough to see them return.

Late in 1812, Charles Cessna took an afternoon nap on his porch rocker. He never woke up.

Peace was his at last.

On September 15, 1812, Culbertson and his brother William S. Cessna enlisted at Natchez, as privates in Capt. John H. Shank's Company of rifle militia. The Regiment of Mississippi Territory, was commanded by Col. F. L. Claiborne.

This unit was assigned to garrison the old Spanish fort at Baton Rouge. The mission was to prevent any English vessels from sailing up the Mississippi River.

The brothers served from September 15, 1812, until March 21, 1813. It took that long for Congress to move a permanent force of regular army soldiers and artillery into the stronghold.

The boys returned home full of bold talk and wild stories of things they had seen in New Orleans. The other young men in Hinds County were jealous.

A second call for recruits came from General Andrew Jackson in late summer of 1814. He was raising an army to drive the English Navy from Mobile and Pensacola.

A company of cavalry was enlisted at Utica. The noisy, hard-riding, rough-living Cessna boys could be held back no longer. Charles Cessna (21), John Cessna Neel (18), were joined by James Cessna, only 16 years old.[3]

The unit was originally designated as cavalry, but the enthusiasm of the men quickly changed their title to *Capt. John J. W. Ross' Company of Volunteer Dragoons*. It was part of a battalion commanded by Lt. Col. Thomas Hinds.

"Dragoons" was a more fearsome and romantic title from medieval times. It seemed to suit the young Cessna men well.

Andrew Jackson led these men on an exciting fall campaign. It carried them victoriously through the conquest of western Florida. Then they were called to rush back and defend New Orleans from an invasion by English general Edward Pakenham.

---

[3] Though called Joseph Cessna in the bill of sale, he enlisted under the name James.

These three men from Utica participated in real fighting. They were part of the Battle of New Orleans.

Swamp fevers were rampant among General Jacksons' troops. All three of Col. Charles Cessna's grandsons were listed on the muster rolls as "sick" at various times. James is recorded as ill from November of 1814, until he was discharged in March of 1815. The others helped him on the journey back to Utica.

A letter to the Secretary of War reports that young James Cessna had his horse killed under him during the fighting at Pensacola. Records indicate that he was reimbursed $75 for this horse. After *finding* another horse, he continued in service with the Dragoons.

James (or Joseph) Cessna never recovered from his illness. He returned home very weak and with a deep cough. He was buried beside his grandfather on the Cessna farm less than a month after his return.

The descendants of Charles, Culbertson, and William Cessna still inhabit the forests of Utica, Mississippi.

Charles, William, and James lie in unmarked graves on the Cessna Farm north of Utica. Col. Charles Cessna rests near them, also in an unmarked grave. Colonel Charles Cessna lays in a peaceful place that is seldom disturbed or troubled.

He has found peace at last.

Made in the USA
Middletown, DE
24 February 2024

50270275R00126